Visible Learning Ir

Visible Learning Insights presents a fascinating "inside view" of the ground-breaking research of John Hattie. Together, the authors John Hattie and Klaus Zierer embark on a mission to build on the internationally renowned work and combine the power and authority of the research with the real "coal face" experience of schools.

Offering a concise introduction into the "Visible Learning Story", the book provides busy teachers with a guide to why the Visible Learning research is so vital and the difference it can make to learning outcomes. It includes:

- An in-depth dialogue between John Hattie and Klaus Zierer.
- Clearly structured chapters that focus on the core messages of "Visible Learning" and infer practical consequences for the everyday job of teaching.
- FAQs to Visible Learning that provide an invaluable introduction to the language of learning and success in schools.
- An overview of the current data set with over 1,400 meta-analyses.

Intended for teachers, teacher students, education researchers, parents, and all who are interested in successful learning, teaching, and schooling, this short and elegant introduction outlines just what is required to translate Hattie's research into improved school performance.

John Hattie is Laureate Professor at the Melbourne Graduate School of Education at the University of Melbourne. He is the author of *Visible Learning, Visible Learning for Teachers, Visible Learning and the Science of How We Learn, Visible Learning into Action, 10 Mindframes for Visible Learning* and *Visible Learning Feedback*, and co-editor of the *International Guide to Student Achievement*.

Klaus Zierer is a German educationalist and since 2015 Professor of Education at the University of Augsburg. He has lectured and written extensively on Hattie's work and translated both *Visible Learning* and *Visible Learning for Teachers* into German. Together with John Hattie he has written *10 Mindframes for Visible Learning*.

Visible Learning Insights

John Hattie and
Klaus Zierer

Routledge
Taylor & Francis Group

LONDON AND NEW YORK

First published 2019
by Routledge
2 Park Square, Milton Park, Abingdon, Oxon OX14 4RN

and by Routledge
52 Vanderbilt Avenue, New York, NY 10017

Routledge is an imprint of the Taylor & Francis Group, an informa business

British Library Cataloguing-in-Publication Data
A catalogue record for this book is available from the British Library

Library of Congress Cataloging-in-Publication Data
Names: Hattie, John, author. | Zierer, Klaus, author.
Title: Visible learning insights / John Hattie and Klaus Zierer.
Description: Abingdon, Oxon ; New York, NY : Routledge, [2019] |
    Includes bibliographical references. |
Identifiers: LCCN 2018058190 (print) | LCCN 2019014181 (ebook) |
    ISBN 9781351002226 (Ebook) | ISBN 9781138549678 (hardback) |
    ISBN 9781138549692 (pbk.) | ISBN 9781351002226 (ebk)
Subjects: LCSH: Effective teaching. | Teacher effectiveness. |
    Teachers—Self–rating of. | Student–centered learning. | Academic
    achievement.
Classification: LCC LB1025.3 (ebook) | LCC LB1025.3 .H386 2019 (print) |
    DDC 371.102—dc23
LC record available at https://lccn.loc.gov/2018058190

ISBN: 978-1-138-54967-8 (hbk)
ISBN: 978-1-138-54969-2 (pbk)
ISBN: 978-1-351-00222-6 (ebk)

Typeset in Bembo
by Apex CoVantage, LLC

Contents

1

"It depends on the teacher's expertise." John Hattie in dialogue with Klaus Zierer

Visible Learning comprises the largest data set of empirical educational research ever evaluated in a book. It has been translated into several languages and is undoubtedly one of the most influential studies in educational science. Our experience has shown that an interview on central questions is helpful in getting an introduction to the core statements of this work. This is why we begin this book with a conversation.

Klaus **For 30 years you have been evaluating the world's most important empirical studies on student achievement. The books that have emerged from this have made you internationally influential as a learning researcher today. What made you commit to this work?**

John My PhD is in measurement and statistics, as was my career until *Visible Learning* was published. As a measurement person we can cross many education topics, but my colleagues continually insisted I anchor myself in what truly makes the difference to student learning and acheivement. Since I started working at a university, colleagues gave me a lot of advice on what this critical learning should look like. Some recommended computers and educational games; others swore to improving the curriculum. Others emphasized the communication between teachers and learners. And everyone had studies (particularly theirs) ready to prove that their method was the best. That made me skeptical. I took a closer look at the studies and began to compare.

Klaus **You were wondering: What works?**

John No, I asked: What works best? Almost every teaching method has a positive effect; that is, you can find evidence that the method improves achievement. Students almost always learn something at school. In lectures I sometimes jokingly claim: The only thing a teacher needs to enhance student learning is a pulse. But I would like to know what can be done to ensure that pupils make the *greatest* progress in learning. This must be the yardstick for any kind of school reform.

Klaus **With the publication of *Visible Learning* in 2008, you have established a ranking of the most effective factors for good teaching. What was your basic idea for this ranking?**

John Yes, this was a ranking of the factors that influence student achievement. It was intended to draw attention to my core message: What matters most occurs in the classroom, where teachers and learners meet. On the other hand, the framework conditions of schools – the school structures or the money invested in structures – have only little influence. Unfortunately, too often the discussion in the education debate is the other way round.

Klaus **That actually makes sense. Nevertheless, you have refrained from ranking in the last revision of your data set from 2017. Why?**

John Too many started to say they were attending to or doing the top influences and stopping the bottom influences – I wish it was this simple. I created the table to help contrast the average effects of many influences as a starting point to tell the story. None of the influences is unique, there are high levels of overlap, and it took me 15 to 20 years of pondering to develop the underlying *Visible Learning* story about this overlap. The more important messages relate to the underlying reasons for the differences between the above and below average effects – and this is a deeper set of *Visible Learning* messages; and it is these messages that matter. The ranking led to interest, but it is time to move on to focus more on the story.

Klaus **In addition to extending the data set to over 1,400 meta-analyses, from which you can now extract over**

250 factors and assign nine domains, what are the most important changes?

John   In 1989, I published my first article on the effects of pedagogical interventions. In 2008, there were 800 meta-analyses and 138 factors when I published *Visible Learning*. Today, I – and it is just me doing the coding – have more than 1,400 meta-analyses that deliver over 250 effects. Of course there have been some changes in the effect sizes as more studies are added but most have remained reasonably robust to the addition of new studies. However, the core statement, the underlying story remains the same: It depends on the expertise of the teacher. Teachers who walk into classrooms and say "My job today is to evaluate the impact I am having on my students" – this is the powerful starting point that leads to the greatest benefits to students.

Klaus   **What happens next with "Visible Learning"?**

John   I continue to find new meta-analysis, refine and improve the underlying messages, and now work with many colleagues implementing and evaluating the messages in many schools throughout the world. The evidence of this impact in schools is exciting. I am also working to have some influence in the policy, parent, and media arena to highlight the expertise of educators as a major focus.

Klaus   **Is the biggest weakness of your evidence-based approach to be seen in the fact that it is always a look back into the past?**

John   Yes, it is based on past evidence, but when you drive forward in your car you would be dangerous if you did not also look back to check that all is fine. Perhaps the best example is class size research. The effect of reducing class size is positive for achievement but this effect is small. The right question is: Why is it so small when all the pundits would claim it should be large? But it is not large. A major reason why it is small is that when we have reduced class sizes teachers have continued to teach in the same way as they did in larger classes – hence little differences. Notice the use of the past tense in this sentence. So looking back can help us understand why some effects are small and give us direction as to how to adjust if we wish in the future to spend millions to reduce class size – to change the manner of teaching. We now know from this rear vision mirror of research how to proceed if we are to invest in reducing class size: Change the nature of teaching to optimize the fewer number of students.

Klaus **It is good that you address this factor: It is and remains a neuralgic point in the discussion.**

John Yes, some critics claim that if I do not understand the importance of class size reduction then I clearly have never been in a class, and other personal attacks. Some claim that surely those influences at the top of the chart would be more likely in smaller classes – you can give more feedback, devote yourself more to each student, etc. So why has this not been the case? Because teachers continue to use the "tell and practice" model that works quite well with 25-plus students, and they still use it when they have fewer students in the class. Indeed, they talk more in smaller classes, there is less student group work, and less feedback when this "tell and practice" model is used in smaller classes.

Klaus **But it reduces the stress for the teachers.**

John Here, too, there are rather contrary findings. Some of the work shows reduced stress in smaller classes, certainly. But what the research shows is that those who are stressed by teaching with 30 learners are often those also stressed in smaller classes. A recent PISA study showed no differences in stress levels related to class size.

Klaus **Don't you overtax the teachers if you blame them for their students' learning progress?**

John Learning always involves at least two things: The teacher and the student, both with their motivations, talents, and background. Of course, teachers have little influence on the basic intelligence of their students but they can have substantial influence on their learning growth and achievement. Teachers can cause learning and we need to celebrate the amazing success so many teachers have in causing students to learn. No, I do not blame them, I honor them for this influence on student learning progress.

Klaus **So at many schools you see successful teaching and learning.**

John That's right! What keeps me going is the number of wonderfully successful educators I get to see in action. My argument is that we have the basis of excellence, excellence is all around us, the job is to upscale this success. There are a large number of great teachers who feel responsible for their students, who constantly question and improve their teaching, and ask themselves about their impact on their students' learning. Interestingly, they often have the same difficult students, teach in the same larger classes, with the same curriculum and assessment demands, under the same conditions as other teachers down the corridor of the same school who have less influence on their students.

Klaus   **Are some teachers complaining too much?**

John   Too many teachers still think that if they only had more time, larger rooms, fewer students, better resources, they would achieve more. I am not saying that these structural issues are completely meaningless. But often what most learners need is not more, but something different: If my teaching does not have an impact on my students, I have to change my teaching. It's as simple as that.

Klaus   **So what is a good teacher?**

John   A good teacher has high expectations, creates an error-friendly climate in the classroom, constantly questions his or her actions and impact, continuously evaluates his or her own teaching, and works together with other teachers to understand what they mean by impact and to evaluate this impact. Good teachers impact on all students' learning.

Klaus   **You also describe the good teacher as the activator of the class and compare this to the "guide on the side" or facilitator of learning.**

John   Right: The idea that pupils develop naturally when the teacher, as a facilitator, sits alongside the student while they construct knowledge – it is a nice idea, but. Unfortunately, there is little evidence that this way of teaching works best. For most learners, the approach is highly inefficient. I have nothing against discovery learning, but often the most successful way of doing this is to deliberately structure the lessons to help students discover and construct ideas and relations between ideas.

Klaus   **A faciliator can do that just as well.**

John   But attitudes and practices differ. A teacher must realize that it is his or her task to change the learners, to challenge them again and again, and to push them to their limits. This "change" is undertaken via the nature of activities and the lesson planning by the teacher. Most students, as well as adults, set themselves rather modest goals. For example, if they had a three in the last stage, the next time they will probably aim for another three or at best a three-plus. The teacher's job is to raise these expectations and help students see success in themselves that they may not have seen alone.

Klaus   **Protection from disappointment.**

John   Perhaps, but teachers must break with this attitude that their job is to create success and correctness all the time. Because those who believe that they are mediocre are highly likely to stay mediocre. The conviction of self-efficacy is an important success factor; our role is to create confidence that a challenging goal is attainable. If we remind ourselves of good teachers, then it is most likely those who trusted us as students, who saw more in us than we did ourselves. And they accomplished this in a fair, trusting environment, with lots of feedback, support, and encouragement. They created conditions a bit like when we play *Angry Birds*.

Klaus   **You mean the computer game where birds smash walls and houses?**

John   Right. Like most computer games, the program always knows exactly what skill level you are currently playing at and (based on your level from the last time you played) sets the next level a little higher accordingly. This goal must not bore you, it must not be too difficult for you, and it must be interesting and not boring so you try, try again to reach the next level. This is exactly what teachers have to do when setting goals – set appropriately challenging goals. Provide many interesting opportunities to learn to get to this goal. And when you get to the next level, the learning challenge is raised and the cycle continues. And so many of us invest in these games to keep learning and playing. We do not stop when we get to the next level, we want to keep playing and learning and exceed our previous level of skills. The attitude of the teacher is therefore decisive for the learning success of pupils. As a teacher, it is my task to support every learner in his or her educational process as best I can, to try again and again, even if it becomes difficult and failure is possible, perhaps even probable in some cases.

Klaus **Is your favorite topic therefore feedback?**

John   Feedback is one of the most effective tools to increase learning success. At the same time, teachers often provide much feedback but it seems to be very difficult to give students feedback that is received and has an impact. Many teachers confuse feedback with grades. Or they confuse it with praise, which alone is not good feedback. Good feedback tells learners where they have gone the right way, where they have gone the wrong way, and how they can set and achieve even more demanding goals. The teacher can provide this feedback by talking to the student, exchanging written comments, seeking dialogue. But the key is what the student understands from this feedback and whether they can use it to move towards meeting the goals of the task or lesson. The teacher must create a climate in which students dare to make mistakes. Mistakes make learning visible, feedback thrives on mistakes, and they are the essence for teachers to improve their teaching.

Klaus **In what way?**

John   A teacher needs feedback about the impact of the lessons. The teacher must always know where the learners are, what they have understood, what mistakes they are currently making. Only in this way can the teacher question again and again and adapt the teaching. That's what I mean when I say "visible teaching". A good teacher must see his or her own teaching through the eyes of the learners, make learning visible, and thereby constantly evaluate to improve the impact on the students.

Klaus **You claim that teachers often don't know how their lessons are received by students.**

John   We know that from many studies. Over half of what happens in a lesson the teacher does not see or hear. That's why they always have to create opportunities to find out how their lessons really work: With small tests, for example, or discussions about solutions between learners, or considering the growth of student work over time. The teacher needs to hear the pupils think.

Klaus **What role do other teachers play in this?**

John   An enormously important one. And they need others to help them. Many teachers have a false understanding of autonomy, and this leads to them neither working together with their colleagues nor working together evaluating each other's lessons. Too often they don't even talk about their notions of impact with others. Researchers have observed what teachers talk about during breaks, and too often they talk a lot about students, about exams, parents, curriculum, school administration, and other things like football. They hardly ever talk about their own teaching in class, let alone their impact.

Klaus **The already mentioned extension of the data set to over 1,400 meta-analyses has added a new factor that emphasizes the importance of colleagues: Collective teacher effectiveness. What's this all about?**

John Yes, this is among the top influences – teachers working together fed with the evidence of their impact. This is working together to moderate what growth means, what we mean by impact, using examples of student work over time to moderate whether this growth is sufficient, and helping each other to see their impact on students. And it needs excellent leadership to create a safe and trusting environment for this to happen.

Klaus **Wouldn't teachers have to learn self-observation during their training?**

John Teacher training has a very low impact on the impact of teachers. This does not mean we need to get rid of preparation courses, it means we have to dramatically improve them. There are some excellent teacher education institutions but not enough of them. At the same time, young teachers are very hungry to learn. They want to do better. I believe that this phase of professionalization is completely underestimated, because this is where the course of teaching can be set for the next 30 years.

Klaus **Can everyone become a teacher?**

John I do not believe in the thesis that one is born a teacher. The teaching profession is a profession to be learned. The most important condition is the attitude of being able to admit that one's own teaching has to be based on high expectations, to question oneself, to learn (with others) from our impact, and to dare to change and improve.

Klaus **If you were education minister of one country, what would be your first official act?**

John I would not start any major structural reforms, but try to implement what we know about esteem and growing expertise. I would want to reliably identify those schools where they are having a great impact on the learning lives of students, form a coalition with them, and upscale this success. My approach would be to forge coalitions of successful teachers and school administrations in many places. It's hard, but it works.

2

Introduction

Visible Learning appears to have influenced education more than many other books in recent years – Google Scholar alone has over 10,000 citations. But this is not only within education: Its influence reaches far beyond professional boundaries and is reflected in the broad discussions in the media.

When *Visible Learning* was published in 2008, *The Times Educational Supplement* headlined "Research reveals teachings' Holy Grail" (although we should note that not even Monty Python found the grail) and in 2013, the year of publication of the German translation *Lernen sichtbar machen*, the German magazine *Stern* dubbed John Hattie the "Harry Potter of Learning". This resonance continues to this day.

All this despite the fact that *Visible Learning* is anything but an easy read. It is a collection of empirical research results, highly compacted, strewn with scientific jargon, and difficult to understand without intense study. This is evidenced by numerous abridgements and erroneous messages drawn from *Visible Learning* which we like to call "Fast-food Hattie". An example: Shortly after the release of the German edition *Lernen sichtbar machen*, a member of the German Bundestag made headlines. After reading *Visible Learning*, he demanded that the German summer break be shortened because it is detrimental to learning success. It is true that the effect of the summer vacation is slightly negative ($d = -0.02$) as was found in *Visible Learning*. However, the decision to reduce the time as such is not found in the book, and it is false because it overlooks some essential facts. First, it does not take into account that the factor "summer vacation" is based on data from meta-analyses from the USA. In individual states, it was first decided to coincide the duration of the summer break with harvest time which can be up to three months long. Transferring these results to countries that have much shorter summer holidays (typically around six weeks in Germany) therefore makes no sense. Second, the demand ignores the fact that summer vacations have other aims, namely spending time with parents, siblings, and friends, time for reading, and time for relaxing and traveling. Certainly nobody would entertain the idea of having school on Sundays just because students may forget things over the weekend. The results show that students may well be engaging in activities other than school work, and the effect is so close to zero that it is as misleading to increase as it is to decrease the vacation time.

The danger of abridgement is revealed as a far-reaching problem. Not only does it lead to individual factors being wrongly interpreted, it also results in the core messages of *Visible Learning* not being heard. Regarding these core messages, the title *Visible Learning* says it all. This is the key element: The aim is to make learning as visible as possible. Without this visibility of learning, education in general and teaching in particular is all the more difficult, because real learning without understanding is not possible. But in order to understand, the aims and motives of learning and teaching must be transparent and visible for all. This applies to teachers as well: To be successful, they have to start with the learner.

Some have commented that "how we learn" is not visible, and indeed often it is not. The point is that excellent teachers aim to understand how their students think, process information, understand, make errors, have misconceptions through multiple methods, and thus bring alive the thinking. They do this through listening, watching, looking at how students are progressing, and in the artifacts of their work.

This is the starting point of this book as it pursues the following goals. First, to offer a simply written and easily comprehensible introduction to "*Visible Learning*". Second, not to discuss single factors but rather to focus on the core messages and to infer practical consequences for the everyday job of teaching. Third, this book intends to underpin the data in "*Visible Learning*" with insights from the non-English-speaking region as much as possible. And fourth, it wants to place "*Visible Learning*" in a larger context. Because, even though it is a milestone of empirical education research, it is not all-encompassing and must be supplemented with further approaches.

Against this backdrop, the book is structured as follows:

1 The *Visible Learning* story: Insights into "*Visible Learning*"

2 What is inescapable: Students and their family background

3 What does not have much effect by itself: Structures, framework conditions, and curricular programs

In order to make this book as reader-friendly as possible, we have applied the following didactic approach.

Every chapter starts with a reflective task intended to activate existing knowledge and previous experience. After that, every chapter lists targets and a brief overview of its content. This is indispensable in the interests of clarity. At the end of each chapter, the most important definitions, core messages, and action recommendations are repeated in a summary. This provides practice for cementing the new knowledge. Finally, examples are used whenever possible in order to establish the difficult but necessary connection between theory and practice. All of these aspects of the didactic approach have proven effective for the reading and learning process according to the insights contained in *Visible Learning*.

Finally, we would like to express our thanks. Every book is a journey; it is not only important to arrive, it is the journey itself that is worth embarking upon.

John Hattie: I would especially like to thank my friend and colleague Klaus Zierer. We have formed a bond of friendship and critique over this past decade, share family details, and play golf together. I also thank my family, Janet, Joel, Kat, Kyle, Jess, Kieran, Alesha, Edna, Patterson, and my granddaughters: Emma, Dianelle, and Ella. Thanks to the many people who work so hard and well in teaching me how to implement the ideas into classes, schools, and systems, and to all those teachers who have grappled with the ideas, implemented them, and continue to see merit in the foundation ideas of "*Visible Learning*", as outlined in this book. Your excellence is what keeps me excited about our profession.

Klaus Zierer: After more than a decade of intensive work with "*Visible Learning*", I have grown fond of it. My thoughts and actions have changed in all my pedagogical fields. To be allowed to write this second book with John Hattie is both a great challenge and a pleasure for me. So I would like to take this opportunity to express my special thanks to him – and I hope that one or two more joint works will follow. No book is created without exchanges with many other people. Against this background I would like to mention all my colleagues who have accompanied me in my work over recent years – above all the teachers in the projects "Schulen zum Leben", "Streck deine Hand aus", and "ProfiLe". Without this critical–constructive exchange which I have always been able to experience, many of the thoughts in this book would not be as clear as they are today. Finally, my heartfelt thanks go to my family, to Viktoria, Zacharias, Quirin, and Maria. They always show me what my work is good for – and when it is time to put it aside.

Melbourne and Marklkofen, September 2018

John Hattie and Klaus Zierer

3

The *Visible Learning* story: Insights into *Visible Learning*

REFLECTIVE TASK

Reflect on what you already know about *Visible Learning*: What is your impression of the book? Is it old wine in new skins? Do you see it as an enrichment? Are you entirely unfamiliar with it? Or does it make you angry?

GOALS AND CONTENT

This chapter introduces the main features of the book *Visible Learning* and its ten-year history. First, the methodical approach is discussed, before the book's systematic is explained and some initial insights inferred. When you have read this chapter, you should be able to answer the following questions:

- What is the research process used in *Visible Learning*?
- What is a meta-analysis?
- What is an effect size?
- What is the size of the data pool?
- How is *Visible Learning* structured?
- What is important when interpreting factors?

Although meta-analysis is a well-known and used tool in medicine, its use across educational sciences is less well known – even though it was invented by an educationalist! It is a quantitative-empirical research method, just like observation, survey, testing, etc. Unlike most research methods, meta-analysis does not deliver any new data but works with existing data. There are existing data (primary studies), re-analyses of existing data (secondary studies), and synthesis of many existing data studies (meta-analysis). Meta-analysis is therefore used primarily in cases where a problem has already been researched extensively and a number of quantitative-empirical results are available. Quite often, these results do not necessarily agree with one another, so that the question arises: Which of the many primary studies is correct? This is exactly where meta-analysis starts: Its goal is to convert this multitude of primary quantitative-empirical studies into one result; but it is just as important to understand the factors which can moderate or influence this overall "one result". In other words, it is about the general message that may be derived from the many primary studies.

Definition of a meta-analysis

A meta-analysis is a combination of existing primary studies on a particular problem and a clarification of the differences among their results.

In light of the knowledge expansion in all areas of science, the significance of meta-analysis is likely to grow in the future. In educational science, for instance, the number of published articles and doctorates has steadily increased in recent years, so there is no lack of knowledge about education and teaching. What is missing is an overview and systematization of the results of primary studies. This is precisely why meta-analysis was developed.

Meta-analyses have a longer tradition in English educational science. When *Visible Learning* was published in 2008, already 15 years of work were invested – collecting, viewing, and evaluating about 800 meta-analyses during that time. These meta-analyses themselves included over 50,000 primary studies, in which an estimated 200 million learners participated. At that time *Visible Learning* already comprised (some have claimed) the largest database of empirical educational research ever evaluated in a study. Since then, several years have passed and work on the extension and above all on updating the data set has continued. When *Visible Learning for Teachers* was published in 2013, there were already over 900 meta-analyses and, in 2017, the last update was published under *Visible Learning^{plus}*, based on over 1,400 meta-analyses, which combine over 80,000 primary studies and the performance results of an estimated 300 million learners (Table 3.1).

In order to put the insights included in *Visible Learning* in the proper context, it is necessary to point out the advantages and disadvantages of meta-analysis. Table 3.2 summarizes the most important aspects.

At this point we should remember that every research method has its advantages and disadvantages, and its benefits must be judged with a view to the declared goal. The pros and cons of meta-analysis mentioned above should be considered with this in mind.

In order to answer the question of what general messages can be gleaned from the many primary studies, a meta-analysis must make the primary studies comparable. To do so, it uses the statistic measure of effect size – usually abbreviated with the letter d.

For example, a meta-analysis might examine the impact of class size on learners' mathematical achievements. To that end, a trial

TABLE 3.1

	VISIBLE LEARNING (2008)	**VISIBLE LEARNING FOR TEACHERS (2013)**	**VISIBLE LEARNING^{PLUS} (2017)**
Numbers metas	816	931	1,412
Numbers studies	52,649	60,167	82,955
Numbers learners	*ca.* 200 million	*ca.* 240 million	*ca.* 300 million

TABLE 3.2

ADVANTAGES	**DISADVANTAGES**
Summary of several primary studies	Problem of different quality standards of primary studies with regard to sample and study design
Increased reliability (validity)	Problem of differences between published and unpublished research results (grey literature problem)
Clarification of the differences among results (variance)	Problem of comparability of research results due to theoretical or cultural differences

group is reduced in size (e.g., class size of 15) while a matching control group remains unchanged (e.g., class size of 30). The effects of these students in these two class groups may then be compared. Or, we could have one class of 30 divided into two classes of 15, and the difference between pre- and post-tests of the learners' mathematical skills before and then four weeks after the class reduction can be calculated. Let us suppose that the smaller group scored an average of 60 points in the pre-test and an average of 65 points in the post-test. Now we take those values and compare them to the values of the control group, which also scored an average of 60 points in the pre-test and an average of 62 points in the post-test. Since the achievement gain of the trial group is higher than that of the control group, this indicates that there is a connection between the reduction in class size and the students' mathematical achievement.

Definition of effect size

Effect size is a statistical measure to denote the magnitude of the effect between two groups, or between a pre- and post-group average.

It would be premature, however, to conclude that the intervention is more effective based merely on the difference in the average achievement gain of the two groups. There can be many factors influencing this average, for example, if some students are having a bad day when taking the test. To make these differences comparable with other studies on class size, or with the many other influences, we need to standardize these differences – and we do this by dividing the difference by a measure of how spread out the students are in these two classes (called pooled standard deviation).

In our example, the standard deviation of the trial group is 12 points and that of the control group is 14 points (Table 3.3).

TABLE 3.3

	TRIAL GROUP	CONTROL GROUP
Pre-test	60 points	60 points
Post-test	65 points	62 points
Achievement gain	5 points	2 points
Standard deviation	12 points	14 points

With this data and reasoning we can now calculate the effect size that is so crucial to "*Visible Learning*". We note the pre-test scores are the same for the two groups, so use the post-test difference as our measure of effect:

Effect size (d) = (Achievement gain Trial group − Achievement gain Control group)/ Average standard deviation

$$d = (5-2)/13 = 3/13 = 0.23$$

With this calculation of effect size, they can be positive as well as negative values. A positive value means that the examined factor contributes to an increase in student achievement. A negative value means that the factor leads to a decline in student achievement. But we still need to ask: What exactly does 0.23 mean?

To solve this problem, "*Visible Learning*" starts from this classification and sums up all effect sizes found in more than 1,400 meta-analyses across 250 influences (of which class size is one). Figure 3.1 shows the result graphically.

Looking at this result against the background of positive effects, it may be said that 95 percent of all influences are positive. In this respect, almost everything that happens in schools promotes school performance. This could reassure teachers, but it should not (if, for no other reason, this means that everyone's ideas of how to improve schools can be defended, as they almost all work!).

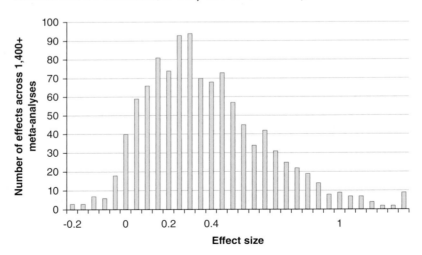

FIGURE 3.1 Distribution of effect size

Against this background we oppose this interpretation of using any positive influence as therefore worthwhile and propose to set the hinge-point differently, namely at the average of all possible influences, which is 0.4. Why 0.4? This value represents the average of all measured effect sizes for "*Visible Learning*"; anything above this average we call the range of "desired effects". Our claim is simple: Being better than zero is trivial; it is more convincing to be better than average.

Another implication is that across these studies, about half of the teachers already meet this requirement. Therefore we do not need to discover new ways of learning and teaching. Expertise is already all around us – probably at every school, in every place, in every country, all over the world. What is important is to make this expertise visible, to take it as an occasion for discussion, and to use it to upscale what is already being done well.

This shift of the zero point to 0.4 is supported when one considers that the human being makes learning progress through aging alone. We get smarter, even if we never go to school, simply by experiencing more dilemmas, problems, and people. These are called "development effects" and have effect sizes between 0 and 0.2. When we look at the effects relating to the typical teacher, these effects range between 0.0 and 0.4, which is why these values may be described as normal "school attendance effects". Any effects above 0.4 are deemed desirable – but we still have to be careful with these descriptors, as small effects can sometimes lead to important questions that help us understand why they are low and then how to improve them (e.g., asking why the effects of class size are so low), and sometimes big effects could be on very narrow measures (e.g., increasing vocabulary scores). Negative values, which appear particularly problematic but rarely occur, are defined as "inverse effects".

The *Visible Learning* Barometer shown in Figure 3.2 illustrates what has been discussed.

The fictitious example above of reducing class size, to finish that thought, has thus far only achieved an effect of $d = 0.23$, which is relatively small, and, in light of the associated costs, such an intervention would have to be carefully considered before being implemented. In fact, as you can see from the barometer, in "*Visible Learning*" the effect size for reducing class size across 4 meta-analyses and 113 studies was calculated as 0.14. How does this effect size come about?

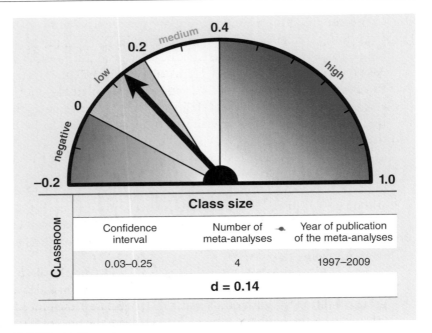

FIGURE 3.2 Class size

There are several ways to combine the effect sizes of several meta-analyses. In *Visible Learning* from 2008 a simple average was taken: For each factor, the mean value was simply taken across all meta-analyses. A number of researchers criticized the fact that smaller meta-analyses (i.e., meta-analyses with a small data set of primary studies) were taken into account just as much as larger meta-analyses (i.e., meta-analyses with a large data set of primary studies). This could undoubtedly distort the overall effect (e.g., if the large meta-analysis produces significantly different results than the smaller meta-analysis). They therefore proposed, similar to the primary studies themselves, a weighting of the meta-analyses. So, the meta-analyses are weighted according to the number of individual studies included. The overview in Table 3.4 shows results for the discussed example of reducing class size.

The difference is easy to see: The overall effect is calculated solely from the mean value of the meta-analyses (using the formula $\bar{d} = \frac{1}{N}\sum d_i$) and gives an effect size of 0.21. Taking into account the number of primary studies in each meta-analysis (using the formula $\bar{d} = \sum(N_i d_i)\sum N_i$), this results in an effect size of 0.14 (because the meta-analysis by Glass and Smith (1997) with 77 primary studies is larger and thus contributes more to lowering the effect from the

TABLE 3.4

METAS	YEAR OF PUBLICATION	N STUDIES	d
Glass & Smith	1997	77	0.09
McGiverin et al.	1999	10	0.34
Goldstein et al.	2000	9	0.20
Shin & Chung	2009	17	0.20
Unweighted Synthesis			**0.21**
Weighted Synthesis			**0.14**

simple average). Statistically speaking, this weighted method is more precise, which is why it is used in this book to take up criticism and represent a further development of "*Visible Learning*".

Based on these considerations, more than 1,400 meta-analyses have been collected, reviewed, and evaluated to date. Against this background (and also in contrast to classical meta-analyses), the procedure is referred to as the synthesis of meta-analyses. With the help of this combination, 255 factors may be identified and nine domains assigned – compared to approximately 800 meta-analyses, 138 factors in the 2008 book, and over 900 meta-analyses, 150 factors in the 2013 book.

The nine domains are:

1 Student with 38 factors

2 Home with 16 factors

3 School with 25 factors

4 Classroom with 24 factors

5 Curricula with 31 factors

6 Teacher with 16 factors

7 Teaching: Teaching strategies with 20 factors

8 Teaching: Implementation methods with 53 factors

9 Teaching: Learning strategies with 32 factors

This subdivision makes it possible to take a systematic look at learning outcomes. It is also aligned with the didactic triangle that has always been used in didactics to illustrate the complexity of education and upbringing.

Based on the actors of learning and teaching – "teacher", "students", and "curricula" – three dialogic structures may be distinguished.

First, a dialogue between teacher and learner in which the discussion about "implementation methods" is to be located. Second, a dialogue between learners and material, which deals with the question of "learning strategies". And third, a dialogue between the teacher and the subject matter, which is primarily concerned with "teaching strategies". It should be pointed out at this point that teaching is always embedded in a certain structure. Consequently, a multitude of other aspects in which teaching takes place have an effect on it. These include the external and internal conditions of schools, which are grouped under the headings "school" and "classroom". Finally, family and social influences should be mentioned (i.e., the "home"). Figure 3.3 summarizes what has been said in a familiar way.

If you look at the data pool for these domains and compare them, "*Visible Learning*" already provides one important result (Table 3.5).

There are some domains that are well researched, such as "Teaching", and others that are less well explored, such as "Teacher". This addresses one of the advantages of meta-analyses: Meta-analyses can visualize well-researched areas as well as blind spots in a body of research.

In the introduction, we mentioned that there are a number of abridgements of "*Visible Learning*" to be found in public discourse.

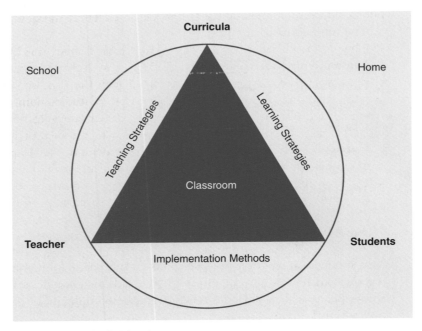

FIGURE 3.3 Didactic triangle

TABLE 3.5

	N-METAS	YEAR OF PUBLI-CATION		N-STUDIES	NUMBERS FACTORS	SD DOMAIN	d DOMAIN (WEIGHTED)
Student	187	1975	2016	13358	38	0.15	0.25
Home	67	1982	2016	3470	17	0.09	0.11
School	114	1980	2017	5672	25	0.10	0.29
Classroom	93	1980	2017	3536	24	0.16	0.28
Curricula	250	1978	2017	11651	30	0.20	0.46
Teacher	62	1978	2017	3406	16	0.09	0.52
Teaching strategies	147	1976	2016	7766	20	0.19	0.55
Implementation methods	337	1977	2017	26192	53	0.13	0.38
Learning strategies	155	1976	2016	7944	32	0.19	0.55
Total	1412	1975	2017	82995	255	0.14	0.37

To avoid these abridgements, the following three steps are recommended when interpreting the factors and their effect sizes:

1. Check the indicators of the factor. In *Visible Learning* in 2008 a number of characteristic values in addition to the barometers are cited: Standard errors (not to be confused with the standard deviation), rank, number of meta-analyses, number of studies, number of effects, and number of persons. Not all of them are necessary for an interpretation of the results. However, the number of meta-analyses at least should be taken into consideration, because this can provide information on how broadly and intensively a factor has been researched. Frequently it is also worth taking a look at the bibliography of *Visible Learning* in order to examine the year of publication and the respective effect sizes in a few meta-analyses and thus to question the range of the factor. If one does this, for example, with the factor "Mainstreaming/Inclusion", one notes that eight meta-analyses are used that were published between 1980 and 2016, but they only take a brief look at a few disabilities. In view of these results and the numerous current discussions and studies in this area, the interpretation of the effect size of 0.36 makes little sense, given that so much has developed since these earlier days of

inclusiveness. In addition to the number of meta-analyses and the time span of their publication, a confidence interval is given for the different effect sizes of the factors. Why? A confidence interval shows at a glance how homogeneous the results from the meta-analyses are and how exact the resulting effect size is. The standard error is used to calculate a confidence interval. For example, there are factors with a small standard error (0.04), such as "Cooperative learning", and factors with a large standard error (0.16), such as "Worked examples". In general, this standard error is now multiplied by 1.96 and added to or subtracted from the calculated effect size. The upper and lower limits of the confidence interval include the calculated value with a probability of 95 percent. With regard to the interpretation of a factor, the following applies: The larger the confidence interval, the more urgent it will be to take a closer look. The average confidence interval across all factors with an interval of $\pm$ 0.14 (due to the average standard error of 0.07) is used for orientation. For the reasons given above, in this book the number of meta-analyses, the year of publication of the meta-analyses, and a 95 percent confidence interval are given, in addition to the factor description and effect size.

2. Check the interpretations of the effect size for and across the factors. Once the first and second steps have been completed, you can form a meaningful interpretation. The comments on the factors in *Visible Learning*, *Visible Learning for Teachers*, *10 Mindframes for Visible Learning*, and the homepage of *Visible Learning*[plus] are particularly recommended, as they provide a differentiated and detailed account of the results of the meta-analyses.

In the following chapters, we will take a look at each domain in order to filter out the core messages it contains. We will select a sampling of factors and discuss them according to the above three-step method.

The first domains are "Student" and "Home" because they form the basis for every lesson. In this respect, it makes no sense to complain about these domains or even to exclude them. The hallmark of the professionalism of teachers is rather to know these domains as well as possible.

Summary

- ### What is the research process in *Visible Learning*?

Visible Learning is a synthesis of meta-analyses, which are the consequence of combining numerous primary studies.

- **What is a meta-analysis?**

  A meta-analysis is a synthesis of existing primary studies on a particular problem and a clarification of the moderators that may influence the overall findings.

- **What is an effect size?**

  An effect size is a statistical measure to denote the magnitude of the influence of a factor.

- **What is the size of the data pool?**

  The data pool includes over 1,400 meta-analyses, which themselves fall back on approximately 80,000 primary studies with an estimated 300 million learners. *Visible Learning* thus represents a large pool of empirical education and training programs.

- **How is *Visible Learning* structured?**

  Visible Learning is divided into nine domains: Student, Home, School, Classroom, Curricula, Teacher, Teaching strategies, Implementation methods, and Learning strategies. The 255 factors are assigned to these domains and the impact they have on learning success at school is described.

- **What is important when interpreting factors?**

  We recommend a three-step process consisting of consideration of the factor name, data review, and effect size interpretation. This process is intended to help avoid abridgements and premature interpretations.

References

Glass, G. V., & Smith, M. L. (1978). Meta-analysis of research on the relationship of class size and achievement. San Francisco: Far West Laboratory for Educational Research and Development.

McGiverin, J., Gilman, D., & Tillitski, C. (1989). A meta-analysis of the relation between class size and achievement. *The Elementary School Journal*, 90(1), 47–56.

Harvey Goldstein, Min Yang, Rumana Omar, Rebecca Turner and Simon Thompson (2000). *Journal of the Royal Statistical Society. Series C (Applied Statistics)*, 49(3), 399–412.

Shin, I.-S., & Chung, J. Y. (2009). Class size and student achievement in the United States: A meta-analysis. *KEDI Journal of Educational Policy*, 6(2), 3–19.

4

What is inescapable: Students and their family background

REFLECTIVE TASK

Think about how significant you consider the impact of genetic predisposition, family, and friends to be: Are girls or boys given preferential or discriminating treatment? Or are the effects of gender on achievement the same or different? What impact do mothers and fathers have on student achievement? What impact do parents have on the values, attitudes, and opinions of their children? How important do you consider the financial security and salary of parents to be to the achievement of their children?

GOALS AND CONTENT

In this chapter we will take a closer look at the domains "Student" and "Home". We will introduce a selection of factors to decipher the core messages for these domains. When you have read this chapter, you should be able to answer the following questions:

- What is important in the domains "Student" and "Home"?
- What impact does orientation along cognitive levels (Piagetian programs) have on student achievement?
- What impact do self-reported grades have on student achievement?
- What impact does self-concept have on student achievement?
- What impact does gender have on student achievement?

- What impact does the socioeconomic status of parents have on student achievement?
- What impact do (other) family structures have on student achievement?
- What impact does television have on student achievement?
- What core messages can we infer from this with regard to individual and family circumstances?

When we look at students themselves to reflect on their impact on their achievement, we examine two domains discussed in *Visible Learning*: First, the domain "Student", in which factors such as "self-reported grades", "ADHD", "Piagetian programs", "motivation", and "gender" are included. Second, the domain "Home", in which factors such as "socioeconomic status", "welfare policies", and "television" are included.

This chapter will look at both domains together, because both lead to the same core message: Both the domain "Student" and the domain "Home" generate influences that have enormous impact on student achievement. Many of these influences cannot be (directly) affected by teachers. The consequence is clear: Teachers are important in the education process, but they are not responsible for everything and cannot be held responsible for everything. And yet, much can be done even in these domains by means of cooperation.

First, let us discuss the domain "Student".

Definition of the domain "Student"

The domain "Student" includes all those factors that take into account the physical, mental, and spiritual prerequisites of learners.

Look at the factors shown in Table 4.1 and consider: How effective are these factors based on my experience?

Three factors are explained that are particularly significant for teaching (Figures 4.1 to 4.3).

Piagetian programs

The factor shown in Figure 4.1 has the fourth highest effect size calculated in *Visible Learning*: 1.28. It is based on Jean Piaget's stages of cognitive development. In this model, Piaget shows that development

TABLE 4.1

	NEGATIVE d<0	LOW 0<d<0.2	MEDIUM 0.2<d<0.4	HIGH d>0.4
ADHD				
Attitude to content domains				
Concentration/ persistence/engagement				
Gender				
Motivation				
Personality				
Piagetian programs				
Prior achievement				
Reducing anxiety				
Self-concept				
Self-reported grades				

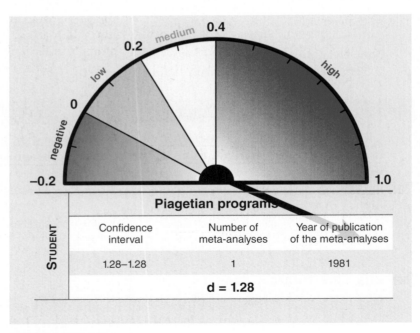

FIGURE 4.1 Piagetian programs

follows typical stages comparable to the stages of beginner, advanced, and expert. This model is internationally accepted. It was also applied to moral, social, and religious development. One point of criticism is the number of meta-analyses: It is just a single meta-analysis introduced in 1981 at a conference in the USA. A cautious interpretation is therefore prudent. But newer research followed up this finding by asking about how the brain grows and changes from ages 0 to 20, and sees strong parallels and support for what Piaget discovered many decades ago (Bolton & Hattie, 2018). The core message is that children go through different phases in how they think – perhaps not as ordered and stage-like as Piaget suggested. The sensorimotor phase is where the child learns about their world through their movements, sensations, and via manipulation, when they begin to separate people from the objects around them, to realize that objects continue to exist when they cannot be seen, and to understand that their actions can cause things to happen in the world around them. They then move into the pre-operation phase when they learn to use words and pictures to represent objects, tend to see the world through their own rather than others' eyes, and while they get better at language they still think in very concrete terms. The concrete operation phase is where they think more logically about events, become more organized, and begin to use inductive logic. In the formal operation phase there is more abstract thinking and reasoning, and they use deductive logic more often. It is difficult for children to decode and learn to read if they are still mainly in the sensorimotor stage, and they will find it difficult to learn algebra if they are still in the concrete operation phase. The main message is that teachers need to understand how students are thinking and processing information, and to construct tasks to help move them into the next higher level ways of thinking.

Self-reported grades

This factor, with an effect size of 1.22, is high on the list, although the results in the meta-analyses differ widely in light of the data pool (Figure 4.2). The core message is: Learners know what their strengths and weaknesses are, what they can and cannot do well. This leads to an appeal to teachers to see classroom teaching as a dialogue and to get student feedback on the learning process as often as possible, but we need to be careful that the students' expectations about their grades are appropriately high, rigorous, and aspirational.

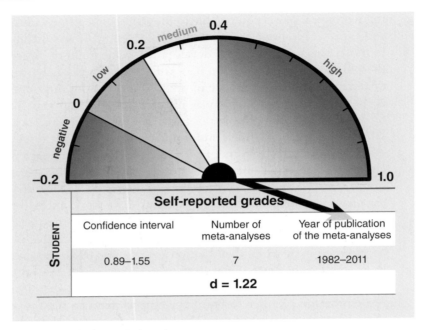

FIGURE 4.2 Self-reported grades

In light of this fact, we should be critical of the multitude of tests that currently characterize many educational systems. These tests usually contribute little to successful learning. More important than tests, it seems, is the learners' conviction of their own effectiveness, which often does not match their own assessment of their performance. If it is too low and the student lacks confidence in his or her own ability, his or her behavior will be hesitant, restrained, and insecure. Mistakes are seen as confirmation of one's own weaknesses and not as a chance to work on one's skills. This is precisely where teachers come in: Their job must be to harmonize students' self-reported grades with their conviction of their own effectiveness, and then to raise these expectations towards higher challenges.

Self-concept

This factor has an effect size of 0.43 in *Visible Learning* – with a confidence interval that reflects the uniformity of the results. What is meant by self-concept? An analogy often used to answer this question is the rope model. The rope model emphasizes that our self-concept consists

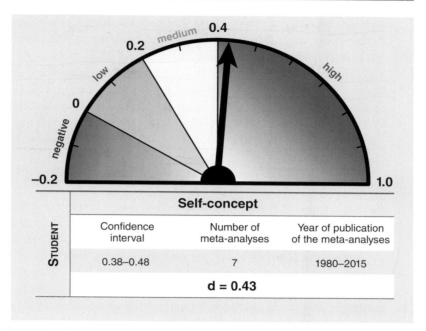

	Self-concept		
STUDENT	Confidence interval	Number of meta-analyses	Year of publication of the meta-analyses
	0.38–0.48	7	1980–2015
	d = 0.43		

FIGURE 4.3 Self-concept

not in a single fiber but in many overlapping self-concepts and that the strength of the rope does not depend on any one fiber extending throughout the length of the rope but on many intertwining fibers. These many fibers refer to the processes of self-concept, such as our concept of ourselves as a student, a friend, a child in a family, a playmate, as well as concepts of our physical prowess, our musical self, and many other selves. In the following, we will go into two of these processes in more detail by way of illustration: Self-efficacy and motivation.

With regard to self-efficacy, some learners tend to attribute their successes to luck and to put their failures down to deficiencies in their personalities, which has a negative impact on their self-concept. Other learners tend to attribute their successes to effort and attempt to explain their failures by telling themselves they need to put in more effort next time. Whereas the first group of learners has low self-efficacy beliefs, the second group of learners has high self-efficacy beliefs. The fundamental notion is a sense of confidence that one can make a difference, one can succeed at the challenges one encounters. Learners with high self-efficacy beliefs have better chances than those with low self-efficacy beliefs of being successful in the long term, because they seek out challenges, put in effort, and are enthusiastic about learning. Perhaps even more importantly, they regard mistakes as an opportunity for further learning. This means that teachers need to be concerned with the students' confidence and their anxieties, since these can be major barriers to learning. By sharing, for example, success criteria that are appropriately challenging (not too hard, not too boring) and showing the student that the teacher is there to assist in achieving these success criteria can increase confidence, allow for taking risks in trying, and reduce anxiety that the student is unable to learn.

Differences in motivation have a similar effect on learning. There are some learners who learn because they expect to earn a reward (extrinsic motivation), and there are others who learn because they are interested in the material (intrinsic motivation). Some students learn so as to appear bright in front of their friends or family. In all cases, intrinsic motivation is superior to extrinsic motivation, and leads to more investment in learning and to greater achievement over the longer run.

Accordingly, teachers need to develop and improve their students' confidence in being able to complete challenging tasks, their persistence in the face of mistakes and failures, their openness and willingness to interact with peers, and their pride in investing energy in activities that lead to successful learning. Before engaging students in learning, it is therefore important not just to take stock of their prior knowledge and experiences but also to conduct a thorough analysis of their self-concept and self-efficacy.

Gender

The question of the impact of gender on student achievement has been discussed again and again – nationally as well as globally (Figure 4.4). It is no surprise that this factor is one of the most examined of all the factors. Although the confidence interval indicates differences in the investigations, the result, with an effect size of 0.02, is small (throughout we have translated this effect into Boys – Girls). The differences between male and female learners are small regarding mathematical, scientific, and linguistic competence. We even see repeatedly that the differences *within* the two groups are greater than *between* them. Male and female students are more similar than they are different. It is neither true that men are better mathematicians and scientists, nor that women are better listeners and speakers of foreign languages.

How can this result be reconciled with the PISA study, which has repeatedly made headlines with the claim that boys are better

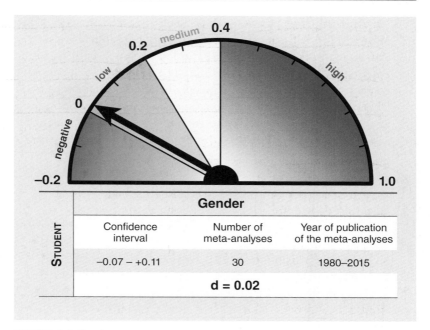

FIGURE 4.4 Gender

at mathematics than girls? At closer examination, however, the conflict is resolved: The results of the PISA study do reveal an achievement difference between boys and girls, but in almost all countries this difference is less than 5 percent – 5 percent of what? That is a small difference. The ranges within the groups are larger. In this sense, PISA overplays small differences: The social behavior of girls and boys may be different and educators may not always treat males and females the same. For instance, girls are sometimes encouraged to solve different tasks than boys, and sanctions are also imposed differently depending on gender. We should thus not have different expectations of boys and girls, should not categorize what students can do as a function of their gender, and understand that every student can succeed.

If we summarize these considerations in the domain "Student", we arrive at two conclusions. First, there are a number of qualities and characteristics of learners that cannot be influenced by teachers: "Gender", "presence of chronic illness", etc. Some of these qualities and characteristics, however, have little impact on student achievement (e.g., gender) and some major effects (e.g., some chronic illnesses). Second, there are also several student qualities and characteristics that can be influenced, and nearly all of these greatly impact on student achievement, such as "Self-reported grades", "Piagetian programs", "Self-concept", "Self-efficacy", etc. The core message we can infer from this is: One of the keys to successful learning is to understand the preconditions. The teacher must try to discover the students' prior knowledge, concepts of self, willingness to undertake challenges, and experiences to adjust the teaching accordingly. Teachers will then be better able to set appropriate goals, select the right content, use optimal methods, and provide appropriate media.

CORE MESSAGE

Learners bring various preconditions to the classroom, some of which can be influenced and some of which cannot. Important for student achievement are particularly those conditions that can be influenced, such as prior knowledge, experience, and self-concept. Knowledge of these factors and the teacher's ability to react to them appropriately are essential.

Against this background, look again at the factor selection shown in Table 4.1 and consider: To what extent do the determined effect sizes fit the formulated core message (Table 4.2)?

We will now consider the domain "Home".

TABLE 4.2

	NEGATIVE d<0	LOW 0<d<0.2	MEDIUM 0.2<d<0.4	HIGH d>0.4
ADHD	−0.9			
Attitude to content domains			0.38	
Concentration/persistence/ engagement				0.42
Gender		0.02		
Motivation			0.39	
Personality			0.21	
Piagetian programs				1.28
Prior achievement				0.54
Reducing anxiety			0.37	
Self-concept				0.43
Self-reported grades				1.22

Definition of the domain "Home"

The domain "Home" comprises all those factors that affect family structures, domestic interactions, and general family conditions.

Look at the factors shown in Table 4.3 and consider: How effective are these factors based on my experience?

In the following, three factors are explained which appear to be particularly important for educational discourse.

Television

It is well known that television can be detrimental to children's achievement levels. According to the synthesis of studies about television, it has a negative effect size of -0.15 (Figure 4.5). It is important to note at this point that this is not a cause–and–effect chain, namely: When a person watches a lot of television, they experience lower student achievement. That is not the message. Rather, it is that there is a slight negative connection: Those with lower achievement levels tend to watch more television, be sedentary, and engage in more passive activities. But if these students do not watch television it may make little difference to their achievement levels – we need to be more concerned with involving students in learning activities, learning from failure and errors, and engaging in activities that enhance

TABLE 4.3

	NEGATIVE d<0	LOW 0<d<0.2	MEDIUM 0.2<d<0.4	HIGH d>0.4
Adopted children				
Corporal punishment in the home				
Divorced or remarried				
Home environment				
Other family structure				
Parental employment				
Parental involvement				
Socioeconomic status				
Immigrant status				
Television				

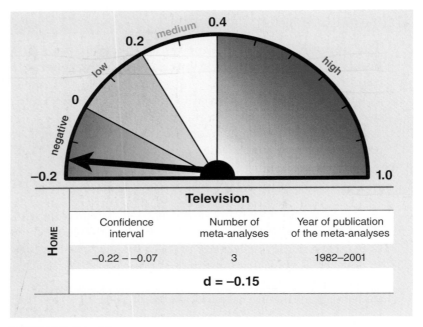

Television		
Confidence interval	Number of meta-analyses	Year of publication of the meta-analyses
−0.22 – −0.07	3	1982–2001
d = −0.15		

HOME

FIGURE 4.5 Television

their learning. With this factor as well, the data pool is not huge, but many studies have yielded similar figures.

Socioeconomic status

The term "socioeconomic status" encompasses several aspects of a student's home environment – usually relating to income, occupation, and education level of parents (Figure 4.6). In line with the work of sociologist Pierre Bourdieu, we also speak of "cultural" and "economic capital". This factor is the subject of much discussion, for instance, in the context of educational equality. The impact of socioeconomic status on student achievement is recorded in *Visible Learning* as being relatively high; in fact it has an effect size of 0.56, which, even in the confidence interval, remains above the hinge-point. In light of this, "soap-box speeches" by politicians and officials expressing indignation at the idea that student achievement does not relate to their parents' socioeconomic status seem to be out of touch with reality. But surely the purpose of schooling is to allow every child, regardless of their parental resources, to flourish, to attain the highest

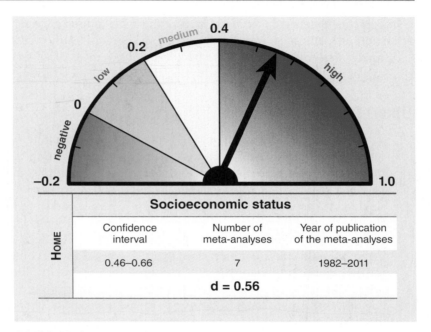

FIGURE 4.6 Socioeconomic status

possible levels of achievement, and not be any less of an achiever because of their family background.

This is also the so-called Matthew effect, a seemingly inescapable "natural law". This is where the rich get richer and the poor get poorer or stay poor. If a child does not have sufficient reading skills by the age of eight then there is significant evidence that they will never catch up. So, if disadvantage, or poor teaching, or lack of resources means a child does not learn to read by the age of eight their life chances reduce.

One reason for this is a core message of "visible learning": Structural changes alone have little effect. Teachers have to bring them to life. For example, if teachers have preconceptions about immigrants, they will hardly ignore those preconceptions just because they teach in school all day. Another reason is also highlighted in *Visible Learning* when we talk about the "language of learning". Due to their limited cultural capital, many parents are unable to give their children the support they need. Sometimes they are not even capable of talking to their children's teachers about education and classroom teaching. Consequently, teachers must first of all try to speak the "parents' language". Second, parents must be supported and given more responsibility. And third, educational equality cannot be structurally prescribed. Only those people involved, most of all teachers, can bring about equality by adopting the appropriate attitudes.

(Other) family structure

The argument that structure alone is not decisive also applies to the question of which family structure is best for the learning performance of pupils (Figure 4.7). In *Visible Learning*, for example, there is an effect size of 0.18 for the factor "(Other) family structure" (e.g., single child vs. multi-child, hetero vs. non-hetero parents) and 0.28 for the factor "Divorced or remarried". The underlying analyses show that single-child families have negligibly different effects compared to multi-child families, classic family constellations compared to patchwork families, or the mother's professional activity. The reason is similar to school structural debates: The family structure is not effective on its own, but relates more to the people factors. This shows that successful and unsuccessful education is achieved in almost every

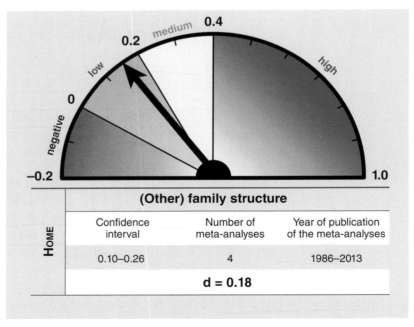

(Other) family structure		
Confidence interval	Number of meta-analyses	Year of publication of the meta-analyses
0.10–0.26	4	1986–2013
d = 0.18		

FIGURE 4.7 (Other) family structure

family constellation. Therefore the competence, mindframe, and attitude of the parents regarding education are more important than the family structure. Parents engaging in the "language of learning" (not necessarily to do with school work, but in many other aspects of being with their children) is a central aspect and may be seen in the factors "Home environment" and "Parental involvement" with effect sizes of 0.53 and 0.42, respectively.

If we summarize the previous considerations in the domain "Home", two conclusions emerge. First, it is not necessarily the family structures and family conditions that have an effect. What is more important are the actors, how they think about what they are doing, what they are discussing with and listening to within the family, and how they make good use of the time available to them. This can take place in a variety of family structures and general family conditions. Second, it follows that parents must be able to transmit their influence as positively to their children as possible – and the unthinking parking of children in front of the television is not one of them. Being involved actively rather than passively in learning, being curious, having high expectations, not being negative about school, and providing a safe and fair environment to explore, make errors, and flourish, are key factors. When this occurs, the home becomes a basis for success at school. Optimum learner support is thus only possible when parents and teachers work together. In fact, quite often we need to start with the parents if we want to reach their children.

CORE MESSAGE

The home has an enormous impact on student achievement. Intense cooperation between teachers and parents in the pursuit of learning, and on an equal footing, is therefore essential. Teachers are not responsible for everything but they can achieve a great deal – particularly when the home is supportive of promoting learning dispositions as well.

Against this background, look again at the factor selection shown in Table 4.1 and consider: To what extent do the determined effect strengths fit the formulated core message (Table 4.4)?

TABLE 4.4

	NEGATIVE d<0	LOW 0<d<0.2	MEDIUM 0.2<d<0.4	HIGH d>0.4
Adopted children			0.21	
Corporal punishment in the home	−0.33			
Divorced or remarried			0.28	
Home environment				0.53
Other family structure		0.18		
Parental employment		0.05		
Parental involvement				0.42
Socioeconomic status				0.56
Immigrant status		0.01		
Television	−0.15			

Summary

■ **What is important in the domains "Student" and "Home"?**

These domains examine factors that deal with basic conditions of learners and their families, those that can be influenced and those that cannot. These include, for example, "Self-concept", "Piagetian programs", and "Gender" as well as "Socioeconomic status", "(Other) family structure", and "Television".

■ **What impact does orientation along cognitive levels (Piagetian programs) have on student achievement?**

The level of prior knowledge and understanding of how students process information is essential for student achievement. Knowing the level of prior knowledge and adjusting classroom teaching accordingly are therefore basic prerequisites for successful learning.

■ **What impact do self-reported grades have on student achievement?**

The factor "self-reported grades" shows that learners generally know exactly where their strengths and weaknesses lie. For this reason alone, it seems necessary to see teaching as a dialogue.

- **What impact does self-concept have on student achievement?**

  Learners have specific ideas about themselves as learners. This may be seen, for example, in how they deal with failure. These ideas have a great influence on their achievement and it is worthwhile to talk about them intensively with learners.

- **What impact does gender have on student achievement?**

  Looking at mathematical, scientific, and linguistic competence, we see that gender has little impact, and any further consideration of the issue can have little effect. More important is the teachers' gender-independent handling of learners' social behavior, which can lead to preferential or discriminating treatment.

- **What impact does the socioeconomic status of parents have on student achievement?**

  The parents' socioeconomic status has a great impact on student achievement.

- **What impact do (other) family structures have on student achievement?**

  The family structure has little impact on student achievement. More important than this is interaction within the family and the associated level of trust and stimulation.

- **What impact does television have on student achievement?**

  There is a (small) connection between television consumption and student achievement: The higher a learner's television consumption, the poorer the student's achievement.

- **What core messages can we infer from this with regard to individual and family circumstances?**

  With regard to learners, we may say that particularly those conditions which can be influenced have a huge impact on student achievement. By contrast, those that cannot be influenced are less significant. The more teachers can find out about those conditions that can be influenced and adjust their classroom teaching accordingly, the more successful their teaching will be. Regarding the home environment, it may be said that it has a huge impact on student achievement that cannot be influenced in any significant way through structural changes in school. Cooperation on an equal footing between teachers and parents is therefore indispensable. Wherever this cooperation for the good of the child cannot be achieved, a teacher's ability to benefit the child is limited.

Reference

Bolton, S., & Hattie, J.A.C. (2018). Cognitive and brain development: Executive function, Piaget, and the prefrontal cortex. *Archives of Psychology, 1*(3), 1–16.

5

What does not have much effect by itself: Structures, framework conditions, and curricular programs

REFLECTIVE TASK

Think about how you perceive structural and curricular changes; for instance, the extension of all-day school, the introduction of detracking, abolishment of secondary schools, extension of primary school up to the introduction of new curricula or even new school subjects. What impact do you believe these structural and curricular reforms will have on student achievement? If you think the impact of these changes is considerable, why? If you don't believe they have much effect, why?

GOALS AND CONTENT

This chapter takes a closer look at the domains "School", "Classroom", and "Curricula". We will introduce and discuss a sampling of factors to extract the core message for this domain. When you have finished reading this chapter, you should be able to answer the following questions:

- What is important in the domains "School", "Classroom", and "Curricula"?

- What impact do finances have on student achievement?

- What impact does school size have on student achievement?

- What impact do school leaders have on student achievement and what impact do they have on a powerful vision of good schools and good teaching?

- What impact does retention have on student achievement?

- What impact does the open classroom have on student achievement?

- What impact does reduction of class size have on student achievement?

- What impact does the use of calculators have on student achievement?

- What impact do outdoor/adventure programs have on student achievement?

- What impact do comprehensive programs have on student achievement?

- What core messages can we infer from these facts with regard to structural changes?

Under the domains "School", "Classroom", and "Curricula" in the current data set of *Visible Learning*, 25, 23, and 31 factors respectively have been collected, including "finances", "school size", "school leaders", "class size", "open classrooms", "acceleration", "summer vacation", "retention", "use of calculators", "outdoor/adventure programs", and "comprehensive programs". The range of effects is wide: From –0.30 to 1.57. By contrast, the core message is clear: Structural and curricular reforms alone have little effect. If one also includes a cost–benefit calculation, many structural and curricular programs seem even less critical. This may be illustrated for the domain "School" with the help of the factors "financial resources", "school size", and "school management"; for the domain "Classroom" with the help of the factors "non-displacement", "open classrooms", and "class size", and for the domain "Curricula" with the help of the factors "use of calculators", "outdoor/adventure programs", and "comprehensive instructional program".

First, the domain "School".

Definition of the domain "School"

The domain "School" comprises all those factors that describe structural and formal characteristics at school level.

Look at the factors shown in Table 5.1 and consider: How effective are these factors based on your experience?

In the following, three factors are outlined that provide for greater resonance in education policy discussions.

Finances

One of the most persistent political demands and election promises across the world is that more money needs to be invested in education. You will hardly find a school leader or teaching professional who would not welcome more money being spent on their schools. The effect size calculated in *Visible Learning* based on six meta-analyses, however, is relatively small, at 0.19 (Figure 5.1). This result is confirmed by international comparison studies such as TIMSS and PISA. They compare nations and show that there is no general connection between the amount of money spent on education and learning achievement. Nevertheless, it would be wrong to claim that finances have little or no impact. First, it must be stated that basic financial support is indispensable for ensuring that salaries, school buildings, lighting, heating, sanitary facilities, etc. satisfy a uniform acceptable standard. What matters is what the additional money is spent on. The problem is that these funds are often applied to benefit the schools, not the people. Material resources dominate human resources in the

TABLE 5.1

	NEGATIVE d<0	LOW 0<d<0.2	MEDIUM 0.2<d<0.4	HIGH d>0.4
Diversity of students				
Early intervention				
Finances				
Pre-school with at-risk students				
Principals/school leaders				
Religious schools				
School size				
Single-sex schools				
Summer schools				
Summer vacation				

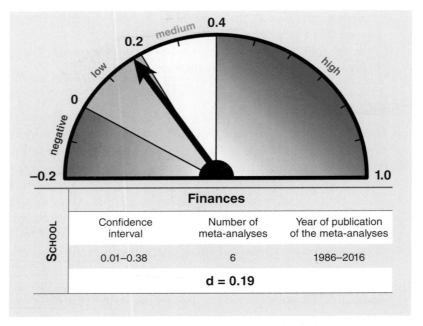

FIGURE 5.1 Finances

broadest sense of the word. We estimate that about 10 percent is spent on buildings, 10 percent on state and national support, 9 percent on transportation and food, 7 percent on student services (e.g., health, nutrition), 60 percent on salaries and benefits, and 4 percent on resources and professional learning. For instance, what is the benefit of equipping all classrooms with expensive furniture or pricey ventilation systems? Not much. It will not change classroom teaching. Here again we see that investing in people is the better choice when additional funds are available. There is a reason why outdoor/adventure programs and professional development have an effect size of 0.49 – we will look at this factor and other, related ones in more detail below.

School size

Time and again the closure of small schools leads to discussions, and time and again there are complaints about schools that have become too large. The question whether there is an ideal school size is therefore obvious. In *Visible Learning* there is an effect size of 0.43 (Figure 5.2). In the search for the optimal school size, a critical value

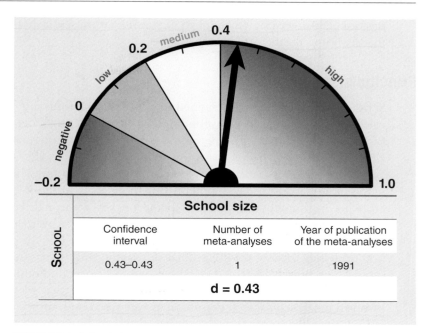

School size		
Confidence interval	Number of meta-analyses	Year of publication of the meta-analyses
0.43–0.43	1	1991
d = 0.43		

SCHOOL

FIGURE 5.2 School size

of approximately 800 students is considered the ideal. What are the reasons for this? This value may primarily be traced back to educational economic calculations, according to which a certain minimum size must exist so that the costs of the overall apparatus are in a meaningful relationship to learning outcomes. If the school is too small, the organization costs consume too many resources, and above a certain size this ratio reaches an optimal value, which cannot be improved even with further expansion of the school. Although these calculations are relevant, there is another, even more important factor why 800 students is about optimal. Below 800 there are often insufficient numbers to offer a similar rich and broad curriculum to all, beyond which there become more electives (which often act like streaming in negative ways to privilege certain students). This is similar to the factor "class size": Size alone is not decisive. Rather, there is ample evidence that the quality of teaching and, in particular, the quality of cooperation among teachers is much more important, regardless of the number of students in the class. The only constant is that in this context the thought "the smaller, the better" does not work (nor, necessarily, does "large, i.e., beautiful"). A decisive characteristic of successful schools is therefore not their size, but the degree of cooperation among teachers, the expertise of those teachers, and the quality of teacher–student relations.

Principals/school leaders

School leaders are often mentioned in the literature as playing a key role. Nevertheless, the corresponding factor achieves an effect size of only 0.28 (Figure 5.3). The confidence interval already makes it clear that there are major variations in the effects of leaders. There are school leaders, for example, who can be the driving force behind school and classroom development. But there are also school leaders who are literally the strongest brake on any reform drive at a school. Consequently, it is not the position itself that is awarded, but the nature and ways of thinking of the person who fills this position and thus creates an effect. That is exactly what meta–analyses show. The school leaders that combine two exciting mindframes are particularly successful: On the one hand, they ensure that everyone involved in the school feels comfortable, well resourced, autonomous in how they like to teach, has confidence, and shows an appreciative attitude towards the vision of the school (transformational school

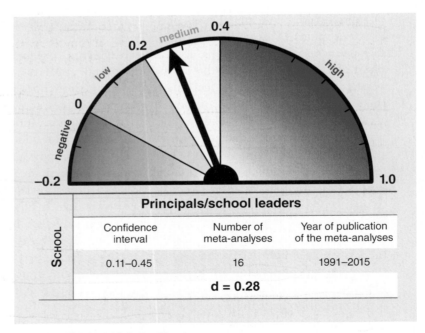

FIGURE 5.3 Principals/school leaders

management). On the other hand, there are leaders who specifically set the challenge and insist on forcing colleagues out of their comfort zone. In light of evidence of their impact, they demand and promote cooperation (instructional school management). It is the latter, the instructional leaders, who have by far the greatest impact, whereas the transformation leaders have close to zero impact. It is not leaders as such; it is particular types of leaders.

To be an instructional leader, it is likely that they will also need to be transformational leaders but to create a climate of trust and cooperation to have an impact on their students. If school leaders succeed in ensuring a common vision about the nature, level, and quality of impact on their students, a common understanding of a good school and of teaching quality creates a sense of togetherness, called "collective teacher efficacy". In *Visible Learning*, this factor reaches the highest effect size of 1.57. It shows how important it is that colleagues do more than just talk about what they do. It is much more important to ask how and why we do what we do, and it is even more important to have mutual discussions about what we mean by impact (i.e., a year's growth for a year's input), who is and who is not making this progress, and what is meant across the school by "impact". It is therefore a matter of making the reasons for one's own thinking and actions visible to colleagues, of agreeing on a common goal, and of living, examining, and further developing this common cosmos of values every day, in every lesson, in every teacher–student discussion. This requires a school leader.

If we summarize these previous considerations about the domain "School", we see a clear diagnosis: Structural changes by themselves have little effect. They need to be integrated by the teachers. Without them they remain relatively ineffective.

CORE MESSAGE

Structural changes by themselves have little effect. They can have an impact only when teachers or principals bring the new structures to life and adjust their teaching methods accordingly. School leaders play a key role with regard to vitalizing new structures: They are responsible for the way the structural interventions are introduced to the teaching staff. They can stimulate teachers' attitudes and opinions, and their leadership aims impact the climate within a school and the effect on students.

TABLE 5.2

	NEGATIVE d<0	LOW 0<d<0.2	MEDIUM 0.2<d<0.4	HIGH d>0.4
Diversity of students		0.09		
Early intervention				0.48
Finances		0.19		
Pre-school with at-risk students				0.52
Principals/school leaders			0.28	
Religious schools			0.23	
School size				0.43
Single-sex schools		0.08		
Summer schools			0.22	
Summer vacation	−0.02			

Against this background, look again at the factor selection presented in Table 5.1 and consider: To what extent do the determined effect sizes fit the formulated core message (Table 5.2)?

Now to the domain "Classroom".

Definition of the domain "Classroom"

The domain "Classroom" comprises all those factors that describe structural and formal characteristics at the class level.

Look at the factors shown in Table 5.3 and consider: How effective are these factors based on your experience?

In the following, three factors are explained in more detail which cause repeated controversy in education policy: retention, open vs. traditional classrooms, and reducing class size.

Retention

Retention (i.e., holding a student back so as to repeat the year) is one of the factors with the greatest negative effect: -0.30 (Figure 5.4). It is common practice in many countries and has been around for a long time. Looking at the data, we notice the confidence interval. Even so, in general, holding a student back leads to lower achievement and increases the likelihood of the student subsequently failing and leaving school early.

TABLE 5.3

	NEGATIVE d<0	LOW 0<d<0.2	MEDIUM 0.2<d<0.4	HIGH d>0.4
Ability grouping				
Acceleration				
Background music				
Class size				
Multi-grade/multi-age classes				
Open vs. traditional				
Retention				
School calendars/ timetables				
Small group learning				
Within class grouping				

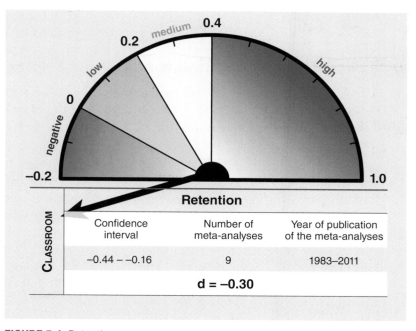

FIGURE 5.4 Retention

What these students need is not more of the same curricula, tasks, and experiences; what they do need is different, and in most schools the only option other than retention is social promotion with their peers. But extra attention is necessary for these students to ensure that they achieve success in learning, that they engage in and enjoy the thrill of the challenges of learning, and that they are exposed to the core notions they may have missed first time around. This means not merely promoting them, but promoting them with specific foci on their learning needs. Holding them back often just invites them to do the work again, often with the same results.

The public education discussion regularly misses the mark on many of these classroom structure issues. Structural measures must be accompanied by concrete actions from everyone involved. This is illustrated by the complementary factor: "acceleration" (which in many senses is the other side of retention). Studies on this factor examine the effects of acceleration on the academic achievement of gifted students. The effect size, however, at 0.58, is relatively high. What is the reason for this achievement gain? At first glance it would appear that a structural intervention brought about the desired success. On closer examination, however, we see that it was not the structural intervention alone, but the teaching that followed. Through acceleration, gifted students can attend lessons best suited to their performance; they are more challenged, and thus become more engaged in learning. In this respect the conclusion remains decisive: skipping a class is a structural measure that can only be brought to life and used optimally.

Open vs. traditional

There is a reason why in *Visible Learning* "open vs. traditional" is assigned to the domain "Classroom". This factor is mostly about structural changes. For example, the studies examined what happens when the front-facing seating pattern in the classroom is replaced by group tables, when walls are removed, or when reading, working, and relaxation corners are established. Although the empirical basis may not be the best compared to other factors, the result with an effect size of 0.02 is unambiguous (Figure 5.5). These measures have no effect on student achievement, because if teachers do not change their teaching style to optimize the possibilities provided by changed external physical conditions, then who is surprised when nothing changes? They continue to teach along their usual patterns, regardless of the spatial arrangements. There is much evidence that when the

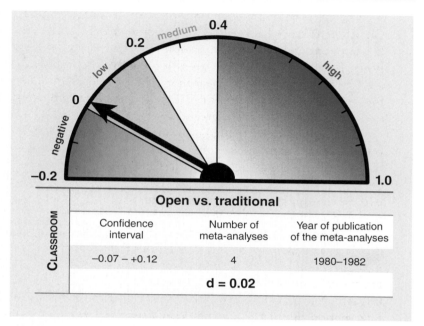

Open vs. traditional		
Confidence interval	Number of meta-analyses	Year of publication of the meta-analyses
−0.07 − +0.12	4	1980–1982
d = 0.02		

FIGURE 5.5 Open vs. traditional

teaching changes, when teachers work with each other to plan, when teachers share students (e.g., 60 to 90 in a class), teach and evaluate, when "tell and practice" methods are changed to more teacher–student collaboration in teaching and learning – all which can occur in open classrooms – then there can be marked positive improvements.

Class size

Most studies on this factor examine the effects of reducing class size (e.g., by 10 or 15 learners) on student achievement. The effect size of 0.14 is also small, which is a surprise for many (Figure 5.6). Almost anyone asked about this issue would answer: Reduction of class size has a positive effect on learning achievement. So how did this result come about? The studies are highly consistent that reducing class size alone has very little impact, because teachers do not change their teaching methods as a result of this intervention. For example, they do not take advantage of the smaller number of students to give better feedback, to have more conversations with learners, or to involve students more in the teaching process. Indeed, in smaller classes they

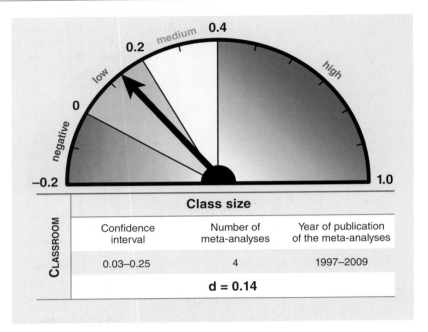

Class size		
Confidence interval	Number of meta-analyses	Year of publication of the meta-analyses
0.03–0.25	4	1997–2009
d = 0.14		

FIGURE 5.6 Class size

tend to do more "tell and practice". The conclusion drawn from these considerations is not that reduction of class size is pointless – the impact is small, but positive. Nor does it appear reasonable to conclude that class size should be increased. Instead, it is made clear that as long as teachers do not take advantage of changed structures they are virtually without effect.

If one follows these considerations and draws a conclusion from them, one can formulate the following.

CORE MESSAGE

Structural changes at classroom level alone have little effect. They can only achieve their effect when teachers bring the structures to life and coordinate their actions accordingly.

Against this background, look again at the factor selection presented in Table 5.3 and consider: To what extent do the determined effect sizes fit the formulated core message (Table 5.4)?

Finally, the domain "Curricula".

TABLE 5.4

	NEGATIVE d<0	LOW 0<d<0.2	MEDIUM 0.2<d<0.4	HIGH d>0.4
Ability grouping		0.11		
Acceleration				0.58
Background music		0.08		
Class size		0.14		
Multi-grade/multi-age classes		0.04		
Open vs. traditional		0.02		
Retention	−0.30			
School calendars/timetables		0.09		
Small group learning				0.45
Within class grouping		0.16		

Definition of the domain "Curricula"

"Curricula" comprises all those factors that implement didactic-methodological programs to promote student achievement at the professional level.

Look at the factors shown in Table 5.5 and consider: How effective are these factors based on your experience?

The following three factors explain what to look for in curricular programs: Use of calculators, outdoor/adventure programs, and comprehensive instructional programs.

Use of calculators

When the first pocket calculators arrived on the market with the promise of changing or possibly even revolutionizing mathematics teaching, there were major discussions, with positions ranging from euphoric to apocalyptic – similar to the more recent discussions on digitalization in education. In retrospect, the skeptics can claim that they were right: An effect size of 0.23 remains well below the bar of 0.4 (Figure 5.7). It is worth taking a detailed look at the data, however, because it turns out that calculators can indeed serve their intended purpose. This is the case, for instance, when they reduce the cognitive strain on learners, allowing them to devote more effort to the actual problem and then to solve it, or when calculators are used as a means of checking one's own work for errors. There is evidence

TABLE 5.5

	NEGATIVE d<0	LOW 0<d<0.2	MEDIUM 0.2<d<0.4	HIGH d>0.4
Bilingual programs				
Chess				
Comprehensive programs				
Drama/arts programs				
Manipulative materials on mathematics				
Motivation programs				
Outdoor/adventure programs				
Perceptual-motor programs				
Social skills programs				
Spelling programs				
Use of calculators				
Visual-perception programs				

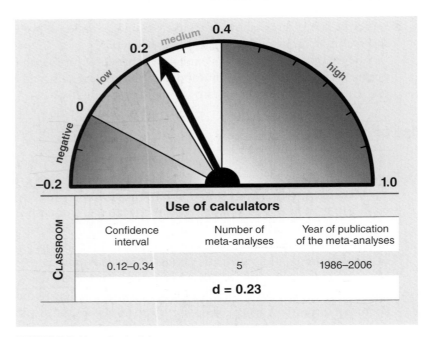

FIGURE 5.7 Use of calculators

that these two uses combined lead to a more positive attitude towards mathematics. As a simple replacement for arithmetical, logical, and spatial thinking, on the other hand, the use of calculators is problematic; but when used appropriately, at the right time, to reduce the load on students so that they can problem solve, they can be very worthwhile.

Outdoor/adventure programs

Programs considered part of this factor include, for instance, extended camping trips and wilderness experiences. With a value of 0.49, they have a large effect size (Figure 5.8). The three meta-analyses are mainly from the USA and Australia. The effects are positive for all areas examined: Mathematical, scientific, and linguistic competence, social skills, self-concept, and motivation. There is yet another characteristic of outdoor/adventure programs: They have so-called follow-up effects and can maintain their impact beyond the duration of the intervention. This is a rare aspect in education. Most of the time there is the so-called fading effect, and after a certain time the impact of the intervention can no longer be detected. This fading

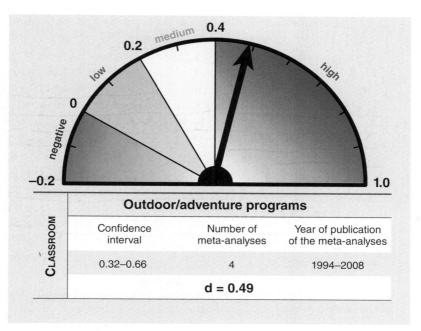

Outdoor/adventure programs		
Confidence interval	Number of meta-analyses	Year of publication of the meta-analyses
0.32–0.66	4	1994–2008
d = 0.49		

FIGURE 5.8 Outdoor adventure programs

effect is observed, for instance, in the factor "early childhood pro-grams". At the end of the fourth grade we can no longer determine which of the children attended pre-school. What are the reasons for the sustained effects of outdoor/adventure programs? One reason is clarity: Successful programs in this area are characterized by the fact that both learners and teachers are conscious of the goals, content, methods, and media, all of which are comprehensible, challenging, concrete, and feasible. A second reason is the teacher–student and student–student relationship, which is fostered by joint activities in a stimulating environment. Cooperation is necessary, and trust is built. We may draw two conclusions from this. First, these reasons may be applied to all structural, curricular, and teaching aspects. They are indispensable for successful learning. Second, it is interesting to com-pare this factor with structural interventions, such as all-day schools, mentioned above. If we do a cost–benefit calculation, the result is obvious: Outdoor/adventure programs have much larger effects and are substantially less costly.

Comprehensive programs

This factor is exciting simply because of its statistics. On the one hand, with an effect size of 0.93, it achieves one of the highest val-ues in *Visible Learning* and makes people listen (Figure 5.9). On the other hand, the underlying meta-analyses differ widely, which is also reflected in the confidence interval. What is this factor and what are its conditions of success? This curricular program focusses on annotated curricula, detailed lesson plans, and a wide range of accompanying material, such as worksheets for teaching or perfor-mance surveys for evaluation. However, this result can only be as good as the process – and here the chaff is separated from the wheat. If teacher teams intensively discuss, focus on the effectiveness of their own designs, and repeatedly evaluate them, the result is carried by an evidence-based approach on the one hand and a common vision of teaching quality on the other. If, in contrast to this, teams find the development of these materials burdensome, the result will lack the necessary depth in didactic and empirical penetration. In this respect, this factor shows that curricular programs alone will have little effect. If, however, they succeed in getting people talking, stimulating the exchange about teaching quality and initiating the search for evidence for their own thoughts and actions, then they can be influential.

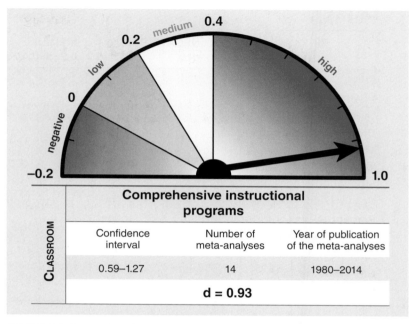

	Comprehensive instructional programs		
	Confidence interval	Number of meta-analyses	Year of publication of the meta-analyses
	0.59–1.27	14	1980–2014
	d = 0.93		

(left vertical label: **CLASSROOM**)

FIGURE 5.9 Comprehensive programs

Which core message may be derived from this for the domain "Curricula" and in what connection does it stand with the teacher? The success of curricular programs depends to a decisive degree on the level of structuring and clarity, and the resulting possibilities of implementation for teachers. This applies regardless of the content, so that conclusions may be drawn: *How* is more important here than *what*. On their own, curricular programs have little effect. They must be brought to life by teachers.

CORE MESSAGE

The influence of curricular programs on student achievement can be great. It depends on how teachers work with the curricula. The more structured and clear the curricular programs, the more success-fully they can be implemented by teachers. This does not mean that teachers need to be slaves to the curriculum, but they can better adapt and monitor effectiveness when an excellent curriculum is available.

TABLE 5.6

	NEGATIVE d<0	LOW 0<d<0.2	MEDIUM 0.2<d<0.4	HIGH d>0.4
Bilingual programs				0.53
Chess			0.34	
Comprehensive programs				0.93
Drama/arts programs				0.41
Manipulative materials on mathematics			0.33	
Motivation programs			0.36	
Outdoor/adventure programs				0.49
Perceptual-motor programs		0.08		
Social skills programs				0.44
Spelling programs				0.58
Use of calculators			0.23	
Visual perception programs				0.58

Against this background, look again at the factor selection presented in Table 5.5 and consider: To what extent do the determined effect sizes fit the formulated core message (Table 5.6)?

Summary

■ **What is important in the domains "School", "Classroom", and "Curricula"?**

In these domains, structural and curricular programs are examined in particular. These include, for example, "finances", "school size", and "school leaders" at school level, "retention", "open vs. traditional", and "class size" at classroom level, and "use of calculators", "outdoor/adventure programs", and "comprehensive programs" at curriculum level.

■ **What impact do finances have on student achievement?**

Basic financial support is indispensable. For all further investments, the crucial factor is how the money is spent. Investments in human resources (promoting expertise) are generally more effective than investments in material resources.

- **What impact does school size have on student achievement?**

The size of schools is relevant to the economics of education. But in terms of student achievement, it is more important for teachers and students to work together within the existing structure. This can be achieved in both larger and smaller schools.

- **What impact do school leaders have on student achievement and what impact do they have on a powerful vision of good schools and good teaching?**

School leaders play a central role – not because a person is awarded this position, but how a person fulfills it. Competence and a positive attitude towards collaborative leadership to ensure that the focus is on success in impacting student learning is therefore essential, and may be seen above all in the fact that successful school leaders succeed in developing a common vision of school and teaching; in other words, collective expectations of effectiveness.

- **What impact does retention have on student achievement?**

Retention usually has negative consequences.

- **What impact does the open classroom have on student achievement?**

The open classroom has little effect, because it does not necessarily result in changes in teaching methods.

- **What impact does reduction of class size have on student achievement?**

Reduction of class size results in slightly positive school effects. Learners do benefit, but not very much.

- **What impact does the use of calculators have on student achievement?**

The use of calculators has a small effect on student achievement. The decisive factor in this context is not so much the technology but rather the didactic considerations as to why and when the calculator should be used.

■ **What impact do outdoor/adventure programs have on student achievement?**

Outdoor/adventure programs have a huge effect on student achievement. They are usually marked by clarity regarding goals, content, methods, and media, which is a fundamental reason for the effectiveness of such interventions.

■ **What impact do comprehensive programs have on student achievement?**

Comprehensive instructional interventions can have a major impact on student achievement. If this occurs, then these curricular programs are characterized by clarity and structure, and lead to teachers deepening, reflecting on, and exchanging evidence about their teaching.

■ **What core messages can we infer from these facts with regard to structural and curricular changes?**

Structural and curricular changes alone have little effect. They can have an impact only when teachers bring the new structures to life and adjust their teaching methods accordingly.

CHAPTER

6

Where learning becomes visible: Teaching and learning processes

REFLECTIVE TASK

Reflect upon the lessons that have brought you the most benefit: Were they open or traditional forms of learning? Or was the decisive factor in how the teacher managed to organize and carry out the lessons? Or was the success of a lesson based on how you had to and were allowed to act as a learner?

GOALS AND CONTENT

This chapter will take a closer look at the domain "Teaching" on the basis of the sub-domains "Teaching strategies", "Implementation methods", and "Learning strategies". We will introduce and discuss a selection of factors to extract the core messages for these domains. When you have read this chapter, you should be able to answer the following questions:

- What is important in the sub-domains "Teaching strategies", "Implementation strategies", and "Learning strategies"?
- What impact does feedback have on student achievement?

- What impact do goals have on student achievement?
- What impact does providing formative evaluation by teachers have on student achievement?
- What impact does direct instruction have on student achievement?
- What impact does cooperative learning have on student achievement?
- What impact does problem-based learning have on student achievement?
- What impact do mobile phones have on student achievement?
- What impact does deliberate practice have on student achievement?
- What impact does matching style of learning have on student achievement?
- What impact do meta-cognitive strategies have on student achievement?
- What core messages can we infer from this with regard to the domain "Teaching"?

As in *Visible Learning* (2008), the domain "Teaching" is still the best-researched domain in terms of the number of meta-analyses. Whereas at that time there were 412 meta-analyses, today there are 632. It is no surprise that this domain includes the largest number of factors: 105. This makes both the overview of this domain and the exemplary selection of factors difficult but not impossible. It is helpful to divide the domain "Teaching", which has been done in the course of expanding the data set to over 1,400 meta-analyses, into the following three sub-domains:

- First, the sub-domain "Teaching strategies", under which, for example, the factors "feedback", "goals", and "concept mapping" are summarized. Consequently, these are interventions that may be seen from the teacher's point of view with the aim of optimizing teaching and learning processes. These methods can often be used independently of subjects.
- Second, the sub-domain "Implementation methods", which includes the factors "direct instruction", "mobile phones", "cooperative learning", and "providing formative evaluation". Consequently, the focus is on interventions which optimize interactions between learners and teachers.

- Third, the sub-domain "Learning strategies", which includes the factors "deliberate practice", "matching style of learning", and "meta-cognitive strategies". These interventions are aimed at students, helping them towards successful learning.

These three sub-domains are presented below, before finally looking again comprehensively at the domain "Teaching".

First, the sub-domain "Teaching strategies".

Definition of the domain "Teaching strategies"

The sub-domain "Teaching strategies" comprises all the factors teachers consider necessary to optimize teaching and learning processes.

Look at the factors presented in Table 6.1 and consider: How effective are these factors based on my experience?

Feedback

Feedback stands out as a special factor – not only because of its large effect size of 0.70 (Figure 6.1). It is also significant that this factor is based on 31 meta-analyses and 1,431 individual studies, which is one of the largest data pools. Feedback is thus one of the best-researched factors of all. However, this should not ignore the fact that there are very different

TABLE 6.1

	NEGATIVE $d<0$	LOW $0<d<0.2$	MEDIUM $0.2<d<0.4$	HIGH $d>0.4$
Behavioral objectives/ advance organizers				
Classroom discussion				
Concept mapping				
Feedback				
Goal commitment				
Goals				
Learning hierarchies				
Planning and prediction				
Providing formative evaluation				
Response to intervention				
Worked examples				

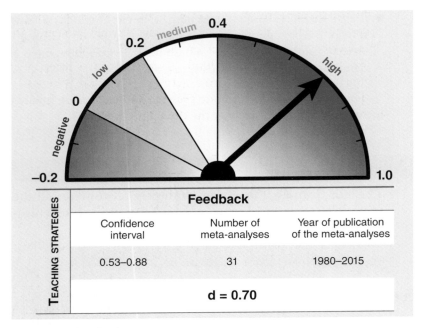

Feedback		
Confidence interval	Number of meta-analyses	Year of publication of the meta-analyses
0.53–0.88	31	1980–2015
d = 0.70		

FIGURE 6.1 Feedback

research results and not every form of feedback is automatically effective. The confidence interval illustrates this. Which type of feedback has consequently the greatest effect on achievement? Not praise and criticism, as in "You did that well" or "You didn't do that very well". Indeed, this is among the poorest forms of feedback, if for no other reason that it gets in the way of feedback messages about our work – we remember the praise and sometimes ignore the feedback. Both are of limited effectiveness, because they only focus on the self and do not give any detailed information about learning goals and the learning itself.

In addition, praise lacks information about how students can control and regulate their own learning. This is exactly the kind of information learners want and need the most. However, as already noted, while the effects of feedback are high overall, there can be wide variability. Sorting out this variability is critical.

It helps if we examine feedback at four levels: task, process, self-regulation, and self. Although teachers give feedback quite often, it needs to be focused at their level of learning (or slightly above). If the work is at the task level (learning content and ideas), this is where feedback helps the most. If the work is at the process level (teachers helping students work out errors, trying new ways of learning), feedback is again positive.

If the work is at the self-regulation level (students detecting errors themselves, self-regulating their work), feedback is certainly helpful. There is little merit in focusing feedback on the "self" (i.e., praise).

Further, feedback at each level typically addresses three questions: Where am I going?, How am I getting there?, and Where to next? In this context, we talk about "Feed up", "Feed back", and "Feed forward". Figure 6.2 summarizes these thoughts.

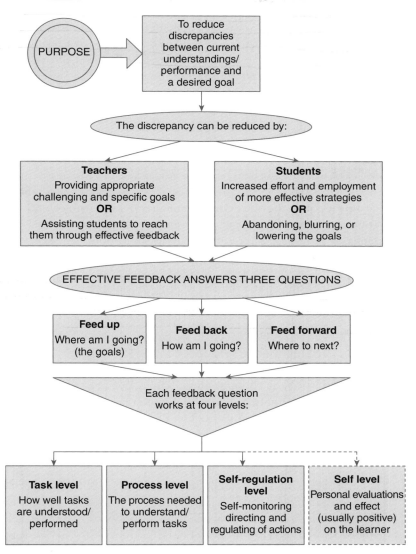

FIGURE 6.2 A model of feedback

Feedback feeds off errors. It is essential *not* to see mistakes as something bad or something that must be avoided. Mistakes are part of learning and give us important information about how to be successful in the future. Mistakes are also part of teaching. If we evaluate our teaching, we see that we cannot solve the problem without feedback from students: The students can let us know whether they have achieved the goals, whether they have understood the content, whether they were able to apply the methods, whether they were able to work with the media, whether they were given enough time, and whether the spatial arrangements were conducive. Once the teacher has this information, he or she can plan the next lesson sensibly. Without this information, the teacher runs the risk of planning above the students' levels of performance. The teacher's own assessment of the process and success of the teaching is not enough. It may actually be misleading: Sometimes students learn how to function in the classroom and play the game – look busy, just finish the work, listen to the teacher. So, from the teacher's point of view, the class may be moving along perfectly satisfactorily, but in reality the students are bored or not engaged. This clearly makes the point: Feedback is important for learners as well as for teachers.

In fact, it is the most important driver of learning and teaching for both sides. Not only do learners but also teachers need an open and academic learning culture where the productive aspect of mistakes may be used as an opportunity for future teaching and learning. The way mistakes are handled is an expression of educational professionalism – not a deficit. Making mistakes is not a problem but a perfectly normal part of learning and teaching. Problems arise when mistakes are not dealt with and are therefore repeated. One of the world's best and most successful basketball players of all time, Michael Jordan, strikingly expressed the connection between mistakes and success: "More than nine thousand throws in my career missed the basket. I lost nearly three hundred games. Twenty-six times it was up to me to make the game-winning basket, and I failed. I failed over and over and over again in my life. That is why I am successful."

At this point, we would like to warn you of another misinterpretation: Just because praise and criticism have little direct impact on scholastic achievement, they are not worthless. They are important at another level, namely when it comes to building a teacher–student relationship and an atmosphere of trust and safety. The crucial factor is that praise and criticism should be dispensed efficiently: not too often, but often enough, and at the right time for the right purpose – but do not let praise get in the way of students listening to and understanding feedback about their work.

Goals

The factor "goals" achieves an effect size of 0.59 in *Visible Learning* (see Figure 6.3). Goals are closely related to several other factors already touched on in this book, particularly aligning with the mindframe "I focus on learning and the language of learning".

In that discussion, we drew attention to the fact that the choice of and details contained in goals are more successful when based on the level at which teachers consider their students' prior knowledge to be. This includes knowing where students are in their learning, how they think about their learning and experiences, what they bring from their home and culture, their reaction to challenges and desire to invest more in their learning, and taking this prior knowledge as the basis for your teaching and instruction. This implies that it may be necessary to define goals at different levels of difficulty for different students, which is an issue we will discuss below. Another important point in this context is that we are not referring to the goals one typically finds specified in curricula. Curricular goals are often too far removed from learners – too far from the learning on a specific lesson or day. More concrete instructional goals are needed to meet

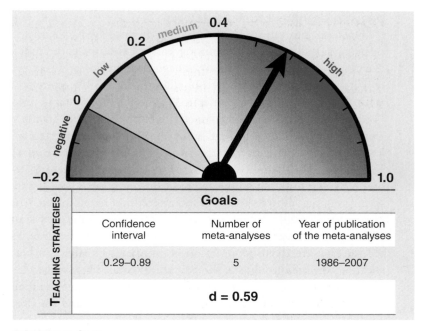

Goals		
Confidence interval	Number of meta-analyses	Year of publication of the meta-analyses
0.29–0.89	5	1986–2007
d = 0.59		

FIGURE 6.3 Goals

the specific requirements students should use to enable them to focus on explicit learning goals.

The most important aspect of goals is that they should specify the level of challenge to be attained in the lesson – in terms of ideas, relations between ideas, or transfer of knowledge and understanding to new tasks. It is the degree of mastery that needs to be communicated. Mager (1997) adds three further worthwhile criteria (although the third criterion is close to our key attribute of challenging goals):

1 They need to describe the observable behaviors the learners should exhibit by the end of the lesson (e.g., writing down, calculating, reading).
2 They need to name conditions for monitoring the learners' behavior (e.g., how much time is allowed to complete the assignment, what aids are permitted, whether they can work together with other learners).
3 They need to specify standards of evaluation for determining whether and to what extent the learners have achieved their goal (e.g., how many of the tasks need to be completed correctly).

To this we add that it helps to co-construct them with the learners but with clear input from the teacher.

This also illustrates why the advice "do your best", heard so often in pedagogical contexts and among parents, is not very helpful in the learning process. It is much too vague, too imprecise, and too arbitrary to allow for a detailed and compelling analysis. For many students, whatever they do they consider to be their best, and sometimes this "best" is not good enough. Indeed, most of the studies in the meta-analyses contrast "do your best" with "appropriately challenging" tasks, and this leads to major differences in the quality of learning. If, for example, a runner (Jesse) sets the goal of doing his best on a 10-kilometer course, how is he supposed to evaluate the run? Jesse is better off setting a concrete time as a goal and attempting to achieve it – such as running the 10 kilometers in less than 60 minutes. This goal would be all the more powerful if it related to Jesse's personal best time. Hence, we see that the goal becomes an appropriately challenging task. In addition, it alludes to one of the key points of successful goals: It is not enough for teachers to be clear about the goals of their instruction. As important as this is, it is only the first step. The second step involves ensuring that this clarity is also understood by learners through reaching an understanding with them as to how the learning should proceed and making the criteria for successful learning visible. Most students quickly understand the notion of one's "personal best" and this is a powerful way of introducing to students the notion of challenging goals.

Rather than saying "do your best", consider the value of "personal bests". At least "personal bests" have a sense of accomplishment to reference our current learning. What have we already understood, and can we learn more or better than that? Andrew Martin and colleagues (2016) have shown that "personal bests" positively predict students' aspirations, class participation, enjoyment of school, perseverance and engagement at school tasks, and achievement and effort on tests. The major value of "personal bests" is that they make the goals "owned" by the students, make it clear to them what they need to strive for to outperform a previous best, help direct attention and effort towards the goal-relevant tasks, create internal pressure to perform while arousing energy and effort, and thus energize students to persevere and stay on task (often despite failure) to reach "personal bests". "Personal bests" can relate to each of Mager's three criteria: showing more or better workings, checking and revising work, asking more questions, working collaboratively with others, using time better, seeking advice about the standards of evaluation of success, and performing better on assignments (see also Martin, 2012).

Providing formative evaluation

Formative evaluation, namely the evaluation of the teaching process, is a special kind of feedback (Figure 6.4). It differs from summative evaluation, which is the evaluation of the teaching result in terms of its benefits. While the evaluation of the teaching process tries to gather information in order to change the concrete situation during the process of evaluation, evaluation of the teaching result looks at the education system as a whole in order to facilitate changes in the medium and long term. For instance, tests may be seen as an evaluation of the teaching process, and studies like PISA as an evaluation of the teaching result.

The data pool, containing only three meta-analyses, is small but unambiguous. Offering formative evaluation to the teacher about their impact has a large effect size of 0.90. The above example of tests illustrates this point: Tests contain information about the students' achievement level following a certain period of teaching. They tell us what the students have and have not learned, where we need to review and intensify, and what type of teaching works. All this provides important information about the learners, as well as crucial feedback

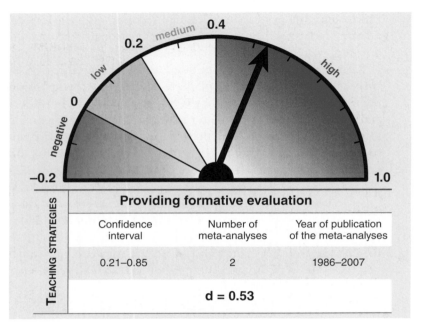

Providing formative evaluation		
Confidence interval	Number of meta-analyses	Year of publication of the meta-analyses
0.21–0.85	2	1986–2007

d = 0.53

TEACHING STRATEGIES

FIGURE 6.4 Providing formative evaluation

to the teacher: Only when the teacher knows what students are capable of and what works well can he or she plan further lessons. Offering formative evaluation to the teacher helps make learning visible.

If one summarizes the previous considerations in the sub-domain "Teaching strategies", it becomes apparent that none of the mentioned factors works of its own accord all of the time. It is always important that teachers, based on their knowledge of the class and the initial learning situation, decide which measure to take at which point in time for which learners with regard to which learning objective – and then to constantly reflect on and review this measure.

CORE MESSAGE

"Teaching strategies" cannot work on their own. They can only achieve their effect if teachers have both the competence and attitude to select suitable methods for the specific needs of the students and to check whether they are confident and appreciative, dialogical and communicative, challenging and stimulating, and to promote a positive culture where errors are seen as opportunities to learn.

TABLE 6.2

	NEGATIVE d<0	LOW 0<d<0.2	MEDIUM 0.2<d<0.4	HIGH d>0.4
Behavioral objectives/ advance organizers				0.41
Classroom discussion				0.82
Concept mapping				0.61
Feedback				0.70
Goal commitment				0.44
Goals				0.59
Learning hierarchies		0.19		
Planning and prediction				0.56
Providing formative evaluation				0.53
Response to intervention				1.34
Worked examples				0.47

Against this background, look again at the factor selection presented in Table 6.1 and consider: To what extent do the determined effect sizes fit the formulated core message (Table 6.2)?

Now to the sub-domain "Implementation methods".

Definition of the sub-domain "Implementation methods"

The sub-domain "Implementation methods" comprises all those factors aimed at optimizing interactions between learners and teachers.

Look at the factors shown in Table 6.3 and consider: How effective are these factors based on my experience?

Direct instruction

Direct instruction, which is a form of teaching where the teacher follows clear goals and deliberately leads students to achieve those goals, has an above-average effect size of 0.45 (Figure 6.5). Looking back, this factor has given rise to several misinterpretations. This is also indicated by the confidence interval. Many equated it with frontal teaching and lots of discussion. This is not correct, which becomes

TABLE 6.3

	NEGATIVE d<0	LOW 0<d<0.2	MEDIUM 0.2<d<0.4	HIGH d>0.4
Clicker				
Co-/team teaching				
Competitive vs. individualistic learning				
Cooperative learning				
Cooperative vs. competitive learning				
Cooperative vs. individualistic learning				
Direct instruction				
Discovery-based teaching				
Homework				
Inductive teaching				
Inquiry-based teaching				
Jigsaw method				
Mobile phones				
One-on-one laptops				
Problem-based learning				
Use of PowerPoint				

clear when we look more closely at the term "direct instruction". It comes from the US education system, and care is needed when it is considered interms of "didactical teaching" – it is *not* the same.

This means that there is a terminology problem which needs to be clarified before the results from *Visible Learning* can be applied. What do we mean by "direct instruction"? Essentially, the method is characterized by clarity on the part of the teacher with regard to goals, content, methods, and media, and the teacher is able to project that clarity onto students. Ultimately, it describes a teaching situation where both teacher and students know exactly who has to do what, when, why, how, and with whom. The teacher "guides" the class through the instruction in didactically skillful ways, without neglecting the importance of students' own activities. This form of teaching particularly benefits weaker students who depend on clear orientation more than other, stronger students. All this can

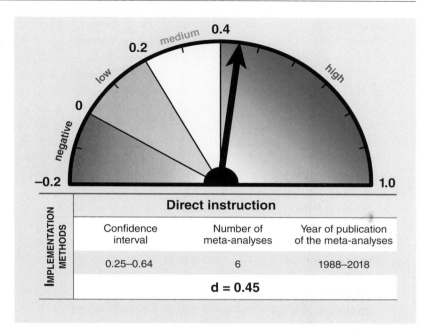

FIGURE 6.5 Direct instruction

be achieved in well-organized didactical teaching – but not always. Equally, it can be achieved in a phase of successful group work. It is a question of evidence: What is the effect of the method on achievement and how can I make this effect visible? In the case of direct instruction, both questions are easily answered: Direct instruction is a method that has a huge impact on scholastic achievement. It may be used in closed as well as open forms of classroom teaching and is characterized primarily by clarity regarding goals, content, methods, media, space, and time on the teacher's as well as the students' part.

Cooperative learning

In *Visible Learning*, cooperative learning, meaning learning together with peers, was compared to competitive learning, which means learning in competition with peers, and with individualistic learning, meaning students learning on their own. The data pool of 19 meta-analyses is large. The effect size of 0.47 is above average and the result is plain to see (Figure 6.6): Cooperative learning is definitely superior to the other two forms with regard to student achievement ("Cooperative learning vs. individualistic learning" with d = 0.62 and "Cooperative learning vs. competitive learning" with d = 0.58). Many believe that this is proof that open classroom teaching is more successful than closed. However, this is another misinterpretation, which becomes clear when we refer back to the previous considerations about direct instruction: Cooperative learning is not the same as open teaching, since it may be used in many forms of classroom structures – and it is especially effective when learners are clear about goals, content, methods, media, space, and time – which is preceded by the same kind of clarity on the teacher's part.

A prerequisite for this is that students know what the task is, what they need to do, and what they have to work with during all phases of cooperative learning. This emphasizes the learning group's effect on the individual's performance in a unique way. Another important conclusion is that studies have shown that the effect size of cooperative learning increases the older the learners are. The explanation is the same as one of the reasons why homework is also more effective the older the learners are: Cooperative learning

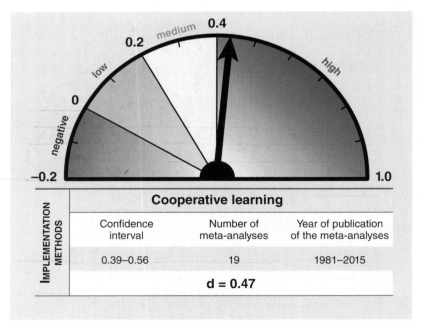

FIGURE 6.6 Cooperative learning

has to be learned. Anyone who has taught at primary sch
how hard it is for primary schoolchildren to concentra
their hands, and sit still, not to mention work together. This does
not mean that cooperative learning at primary level makes no sense.
Quite the contrary: We can lay the foundation in primary school
for the later success of cooperative learning. This, incidentally, may
be said of every method: The better learners know a method, the
more it can benefit them.

Problem-based learning

"Problem-based learning", a method that involves using a problem
to present learning material, originated in the tradition of focusing
instruction more strongly on the learner. It has a mediocre effect at 0.33
(Figure 6.7). But a major reason for this lower than expected effect is
that problem-based learning is often introduced too early – before the
students have the necessary content with which they need to engage in
problem thinking. The meta-analyses demonstrate that problem-based
learning can indeed have a huge impact on student performance if it is

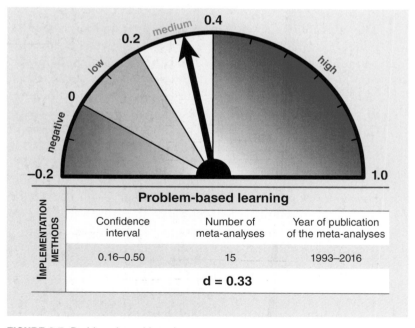

FIGURE 6.7 Problem-based learning

implemented at the right time in the learning process. The right time is not while students are still in the domain of surface understanding (i.e., learning content and ideas), where problem-based learning can even have a negative effect, but once they have reached the domain of deep understanding then problem-based learning will be more effective. In other words, problem-based learning will have an effect only if students have already acquired the necessary knowledge base to complete tasks at the levels of relating ideas, transfer, and problem solving. In addition, it requires that teachers possess not only the competence to identify the learning levels of the students at the start and then assign them appropriate problems, but also the right mindframes to lead the learners into the domain of deep understanding and motivate them to work on problems. Focusing on problems is undoubtedly an exceptional approach from a pedagogical standpoint, because it has fundamental effects on building a positive culture of mistakes – a valuable part of the feedback process – as well as on learners' self-regulation, and on possibilities for dividing up the class into groups. Whether problem-based learning is effective, therefore, depends on several aspects, and it is one of many methods teachers can implement on the basis of evidence.

Mobile phones

The most influential mass medium today is undoubtedly the smartphone. Nearly every teenager has one, and it is becoming more common to see them in the hands of younger children. The idea of using smartphones for instructional purposes seems only logical and has indeed been addressed increasingly by educational research in recent years. In *Visible Learning*, a total of four meta-analyses on this issue have been evaluated in the past ten years. Although the primary studies highlight a number of sensible possibilities for integrating smartphones into instruction, the effect size of 0.39 calculated for this factor remains just below the bar of 0.4 (Figure 6.8). Smartphones present opportunities for successful learning in that they may be used to access additional information that is helpful for subsequent pedagogical interactions. They may be used to record homework assignments, and to ask other students or teachers questions about their work (many students are more likely to ask questions and seek help via social media compared to raising their hands in class).

One example is obtaining feedback, whether formatively as feedback on a lesson or summatively as feedback on the learner's achievement

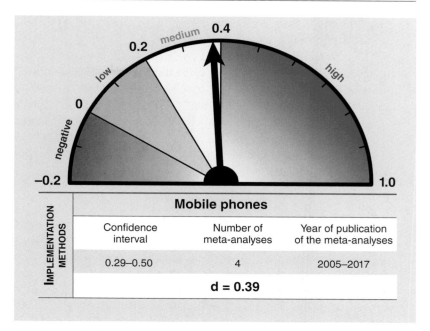

FIGURE 6.8 Mobile phones

level (cf. www.visiblefeedback.com; Zierer & Wiesniewski, 2018). The teacher can easily take up this feedback and implement it during the next lesson. Despite these possibilities, however, it is also important to point out the limitations of smartphones in the classroom, and which are discussed in the study "Brain Drain" by Adrian F. Ward and colleagues (2017). They conclude that the mere presence of a smartphone leads to a loss of attentional resources and consequently to a reduction in performance. Attention and performance improve only when students no longer have access to their smartphones. Smartphones can therefore not only facilitate but also impede learning. Accordingly, smartphone use should be a central topic of media education. It is the use more than the presence or not of smartphones that matters.

If one summarizes the previous considerations in the sub-domain "Implementation methods", it becomes apparent here, too, that none of the mentioned factors works of its own accord. Consequently, it is important that teachers use their knowledge of the class and the initial learning situation to decide which measure to take at which point in time for which learner with regard to which learning objective. They can then constantly reflect on and check this measure.

CORE MESSAGE

The sub-domain "Implementation methods" does not work of its own accord. Such factors can only be effective if teachers have both the competence and attitude to select suitable methods against the relevant background and check whether they are confident and appreciative, dialogical and communicative, challenging and stimulating and to promote a positive culture where errors are seen as opportunities to learn.

Against this background, look again at the factor selection presented in Table 6.3 and consider: To what extent do the determined effect sizes fit the formulated core message (Table 6.4)?

Finally, to the sub-domain "Learning strategies".

TABLE 6.4

	NEGATIVE $d<0$	LOW $0<d<0.2$	MEDIUM $0.2<d<0.4$	HIGH $d>0.4$
Clicker		0.17		
Co-/team teaching	0.07			
Competitive vs. individualistic learning			0.27	
Cooperative learning				0.47
Cooperative vs. competitive learning				0.58
Cooperative vs. individualistic learning				0.62
Direct instruction				0.45
Discovery-based teaching			0.27	
Homework			0.32	
Inductive teaching				0.58
Inquiry-based teaching				0.41
Jigsaw method				1.20
Mobile phones			0.39	
One-on-one laptops		0.16		
Problem-based learning			0.33	
Use of PowerPoint			0.26	

Definition of the sub-domain "Learning strategies"

The sub-domain "Learning strategies" comprises all those factors that can be carried out from the learners' point of view to optimize their learning success.

Look at the factors listed in Table 6.5 and consider: How effective are these factors based on my experience?

Deliberate practice

Even though many learners continue to believe that they can do everything instantly, it is one of the oldest insights about teaching that practice is important for learning success. The large effect size of 0.49 calculated in *Visible Learning* was based on three meta-analyses

TABLE 6.5

	NEGATIVE $d<0$	LOW $0<d<0.2$	MEDIUM $0.2<d<0.4$	HIGH $d>0.4$
Deliberate practice				
Elaboration and organization				
Evaluation and reflection				
Help seeking				
Imagery				
Individualized instruction				
Interleaved practice				
Matching style of learning				
Meta-cognitive strategies				
Outlining and transforming				
Self-reported grades				
Self-verbalization/ self-questioning				
Spaced vs. mass practice				
Strategy monitoring				
Strategy to integrate with prior knowledge				
Student-centered teaching				
Student control over learning				
Study skills				
Summarization				

(Figure 6.9). However, the confidence interval, which is the result of different focal points of the meta-analyses, is surprising: Not all practice is equal. In this sense, the data already show that not every practice is successful, but it must be a *deliberate* practice. This kind of practice is characterized by three aspects. First, conscious practice is challenging. It starts at the learner's knowledge level and sets the degree of difficulty sufficiently high that the learner is just about able to complete the task. Second, deliberate practice is varied. It has nothing to do with drilling or making the exercise dull, where content is repeated monotonously and without thought. Drill may be helpful at lower levels of difficulty, but deeper understanding requires a variety of tasks and higher levels of interest. Third, deliberate practice is regular. Although there are different opinions about how often a task needs to be practiced before it is permanently stored in our long-term memory and available for recall, there is consensus that repetition is important, and that spaced practice is more effective than bundled practice (i.e., spacing out the opportunities for deliberate practice rather than cramming them together). Practice demands concentration, effort, and endurance from learners as well as skills by the teacher to make it interesting and worthwhile.

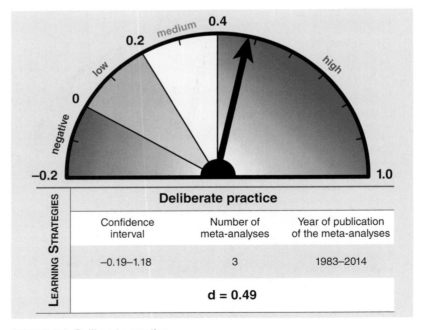

FIGURE 6.9 Deliberate practice

The power of deliberate practice is well known in sports and music, so it should not be ignored in the classroom. Teachers have an essential responsibility to facilitate deliberate practice that is varied, challenging, and regular. If they can do that, they will receive a range of feedback. For example, the teacher will receive information from learners about what they have and have not understood, and learners will receive help from the teacher in the form of supplementary explanations.

Matching style of learning

One of the frequent claims we read in students' research papers, and one which we stumble upon occasionally in the literature, is that students retain 10 percent of what they read, 20 percent of what they hear, 30 percent of what they see, 50 percent of what they see and hear, 70 percent of what they present, and 90 percent of what they do (Figure 6.10). These figures may sound plausible at first, but they have no basis in empirical findings: Not a single study provides evidence for them. If we take a closer look, we will be forced to admit that it is not even conceivable that a study could produce such clear evidence. Even the obvious objection that it must also depend on what learners

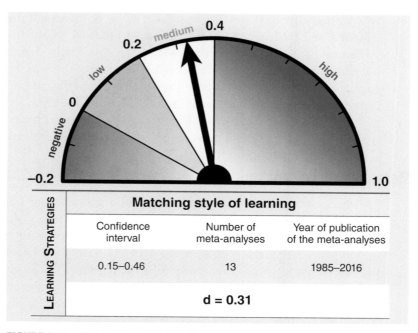

FIGURE 6.10 Matching style of learning

read, what they hear, what they see, what they see and hear, and what they present and do should make us skeptical of this claim.

All the same, there is (or was) a long-established tradition in empirical educational research which attempts to produce these or similar learning style figures. In retrospect, one might say that the temptation to revolutionize learning, or perhaps also the prospect of making a lot of money, was evidently too great.

There are often arguments made that we should understand the students' preferred style of learning and match the instruction to this. In the original edition of *Visible Learning*, the effect of these methods was about 0.3 to 0.4, but further analyses of some of the meta-studies showed they were faulty and could not be used. Hence, in the next edition, the effects dropped to close to zero – there is just no support for the matching learning styles. There is no defense for classifying students into styles; indeed, we should do the opposite, namely provide students with many strategies for learning, teach them when to use a particular strategy, how to try out an alternative strategy if the first one does not work, and understand that students can have many ways of learning – and we as teachers should use different ways to teach our students – but we should never classify students into styles.

If we wish to gain an overall message from this research tradition, we might say the following. Learning is effective to the extent that it is enjoyable and challenging, and the best way to make it enjoyable is not by ensuring that particular conditions have been met but by designing a learning situation which takes up the thread of the learners' prior knowledge and experiences, ties in with their existing thinking, and thereby presents them with a challenge. In a nutshell, when we learn, we gain pleasure from this success – thus learning breeds pleasure. Engagement typically follows, but does not necessarily precede, success in learning.

Meta-cognitive strategies

"Meta-cognition" is a term for thinking about one's own thought processes. The associated factor "meta-cognitive strategies" has an effect size of 0.52 (Figure 6.11). Much more important than this ranking, however, is the message from research in this area: Questioning one's own learning, attempting to make learning visible to oneself, and using mistakes to reflect upon the structure and coherence of one's own action – all of this is highly influential for learning, because it fosters dialogue between learners and teachers. The attempt to reflect upon how we think and learn leads to a critical examination of learning and teaching, makes that which one understands

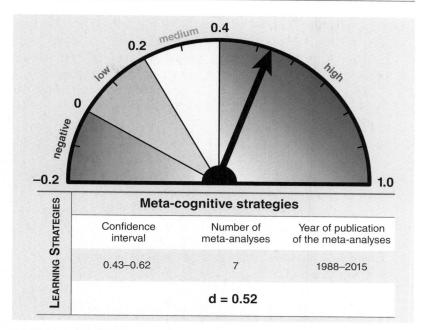

FIGURE 6.11 Meta-cognitive strategies

and does not yet understand visible, and thus provides indications on how to plan the next lesson. Students who are able to self-regulate in these ways are very good at seeking and using feedback. A major aim, therefore, is to teach students these skills in seeking and interpreting feedback so that it becomes a necessary part of how they learn.

If one summarizes the previous considerations in the sub-domain "Learning strategies", a formula emerges which appears time and again in *Visible Learning* (Figure 6.12).

Successful learning is not only a matter for the teacher. Much also depends on the learners, especially on how they manage to take their learning into their own hands with the support of the teacher.

CORE MESSAGE

"Learning strategies" do not work on their own. They can only achieve their effect if learners have both the competence and the attitude to select suitable methods for themselves and to check whether they can use those methods to control their learning effectively. Teacher guidance is necessary to enable learners to do so.

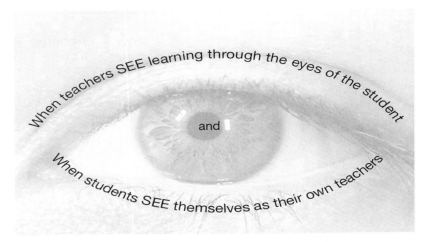

FIGURE 6.12 A model of visible teaching – *Visible Learning*

Against this background, look again at the factor selection presented in Table 6.5 and consider: To what extent do the determined effect sizes fit the formulated core message (Table 6.6)?

Which core message can be derived from this for the domain "Teaching"? In what connection is this related to the teacher? The success of the lessons depends to a decisive degree on the competence of the teachers, above all on their ability to define goals appropriately and clearly. If this is achieved, almost any method can be successful. In this respect, a dispute about methods that can be pursued, for example, between supporters of open teaching and supporters of closed teaching, is not the decisive topic. More important is the question: How effective are the methods used for school performance and how can this effectiveness be proven? These questions can only be answered by the learners. Feedback is thus a key factor for *Visible Learning* and successful teaching. If it turns out that a method does not work and the pupils do not learn anything, another method must be used and how this relates to teaching selected. The excuse that it was the learner's fault cannot be combined with pedagogical professionalism. Likewise, it is not a sign of professionalism to argue that a certain method or medium is in vogue. The starting point and goal of all professional decisions of teachers are the learners. This also shows that teachers need a broad spectrum of methods, and they must be able to use them in a reflective and evidence-based manner.

With regard to teachers, the following conclusion may be drawn against this background.

TABLE 6.6

	NEGATIVE d<0	LOW 0<d<0.2	MEDIUM 0.2<d<0.4	HIGH d>0.4
Deliberate practice				0.49
Elaboration and organization				0.75
Evaluation and reflection				0.75
Help seeking				0.66
Imagery				0.45
Individualized instruction			0.23	
Interleaved practice			0.21	
Matching style of learning			0.31	
Meta-cognitive strategies				0.52
Outlining and transforming				0.75
Self-reported grades				1.22
Self-verbalization/self- questioning				0.62
Spaced vs. mass practice				0.48
Strategy monitoring				0.54
Strategy to integrate with prior knowledge				0.93
Student-centered teaching			0.35	
Student control over learning		0.02		
Study skills				0.46
Summarization				0.90

CORE MESSAGE

The influence of the sub-domains "Teaching strategies", "Implementation methods", and "Learning strategies" on student achievement can be significant. Much depends on the teachers. First, they need to draw upon a broad spectrum of methods, and second, they must have the competence to test their methods for effectiveness. In short, an evidence-based method diversity instead of the traditionalist method dispute. And: To promote a positive culture where errors are seen as opportunities to learn.

The quintessence of the considerations on factors from the comprehensive field of teaching is as follows.

CORE MESSAGE

The factors from the domain "Teaching" can be helpful if they:

- consider the initial learning situation,
- challenge,
- help with self-regulation,
- build trust,
- make errors visible,
- initiate discussions about students' learning processes.

Summary

- **What are the sub-domains "Teaching strategies", "Implementation strategies", and "Learning strategies" about?**

  The sub-domains of "Teaching" are "Teaching strategies", "Implementation methods", and "Learning strategies". They include factors that may be used to, first, control and optimize teaching from the teacher's point of view (e.g., the factor "goals"), second, to make the interaction between learner and teacher effective (e.g., the factor "feedback"), and third, to show learners effective possibilities of self-control and self-regulation (e.g., the factor "meta-cognitive strategies").

- **What impact does feedback have on student achievement?**

  Feedback is a key factor – not only because it has a profound impact on student achievement, but also because it is linked to many other factors: Direct instruction, teacher–student relationship, evaluation of the teaching process (formative evaluation), and much more. The decisive factor for successful feedback is that it refers to the levels of the task and the process and self-regulation, and thus answers three questions: Where are you going? How are you getting there? Where do you go next? Such feedback is important for both learners and teachers.

- **What impact do goals have on student achievement?**

  Goals are crucial for learning success. They must be formulated in such a way that they set challenges and make those challenges visible.

- **What impact does providing formative evaluation by teachers have on student achievement?**

The evaluation of the teaching process is a special kind of feedback. It is important not only for learners, but above all for the teacher, and thus has a huge influence on school performance. Ultimately, it provides the information to make learning visible and to plan lessons.

- **What impact does direct instruction have on student achievement?**

Direct instruction has a huge influence on learners' school performance. It should not be confused or equated with any frontal instruction. Rather, direct instruction is characterized by clarity in terms of objectives, content, methods, and media, both on the part of learners and of teachers.

- **What impact does cooperative learning have on student achievement?**

Cooperative learning is individual learning and learning in competition with other students, and thus has a profound influence on student achievement. It is particularly effective when used in combination with direct instruction.

- **What impact does problem-based learning have on student achievement?**

Problem-based learning can be very important for learning success. The didactic point in time is decisive: If it is used too early in the learning process, it leads to excessive demands.

- **What impact do mobile phones have on student achievement?**

Mobile phones are a good example of digital media. This shows that they do not have a positive effect of their own accord, but always open up opportunities and entail risks. This applies in particular to learning in school contexts.

- **What impact does deliberate practice have on student achievement?**

Conscious practice is a key to learning success. It is characterized by regularity, diversity, and challenge.

- **What impact does the matching style of learning have on student achievement?**

Since the question of learning styles is empirically controversial, it does not seem very effective to adapt learning to them.

- **What impact do meta-cognitive strategies have on student achievement?**

Meta-cognitive strategies have a huge influence on learning performance. They reinforce the core message that teaching must be about making learners their own teachers step by step.

- **What core messages can be derived with regard to teachers and the domain "Teaching"?**

Whether factors from the domain "Teaching" have an effect depends in a special way on the professionalism of the teacher: How does it succeed in selecting suitable methods against the relevant background and in checking whether teachers make learning trustworthy and appreciative, dialogical and communicative, challenging and stimulating, and to promote a positive culture where errors are seen as opportunities to learn? In addition to appropriate competences, appropriate attitudes are also necessary for this – mindframes matter.

References

Mager, R. (1997). *Preparing instructional objectives: A critical tool in the effective performance*. London: Kogan Page.

Martin, A.J. (2012). The role of personal best (PB) goals in the achievement and behavioral engagement of students with ADHD and students without ADHD. *Contemporary Educational Psychology, 37*(2), 91–105.

Martin, A.J., Collie, R.J., Mok, M., & McInerney, D.M. (2016). Personal best (PB) goal structure, individual PB goals, engagement, and achievement: A study of Chinese- and English-speaking background students in Australian schools. *British Journal of Educational Psychology, 86*(1), 75–91.

Ward, A.F., Duke, K., Gneezy, A., & Bos, M.W. (2017). Brain drain: The mere presence of one's own smartphone reduces available cognitive capacity. *Journal of the Association for Consumer Research, 2*(2), 140–154.

Zierer, K., & Wisniewski, B. (2018): *Using student feedback for successful teaching*. Abingdon, Oxon: Routledge.

7

What really matters: Teachers and their passion

The core messages in the previous domains "Student", "Home", "School", "Classroom", and "Teaching" emphasized the role of teachers. In this respect, the question is raised as to what distinguishes successful teachers. A look at the domain "Teacher" provides information on this question.

Definition of the domain "Teacher"

The domain "Teacher" comprises all those factors that analyze the competences and attitudes of teachers regarding subject matter, and didactic and pedagogical aspects.

Look at the factors presented in Table 7.1 and consider: How effective are these factors based on your experience?

What is interesting for this domain is that, together with the domain "Home", it is the least researched area, but at the same time

TABLE 7.1

	NEGATIVE d<0	LOW 0<d<0.2	MEDIUM 0.2<d<0.4	HIGH d>0.4
Micro-teaching				
Professional development				
Student rating of quality of teaching				
Teacher clarity				
Teacher credibility				
Teacher education				
Teacher effects				
Teacher estimates of achievement				
Teacher expectations				
Teacher performance pay				
Teacher personality				
Teacher subject matter knowledge				
Teacher verbal ability				
Teacher–student relationships				
Teachers not labeling students				
Teaching communication skills and strategies				

also the most influential. It contains 16 factors, 10 of which have an effect size greater than 0.4. The factors "teacher subject matter knowledge", "professional development", "teacher–student relationships", and "teacher clarity" are explained below. They help crystallize the core message of this domain. The first is "teacher subject matter knowledge", which is always up for discussion. The low effect size of 0.10 is one of the main reasons.

Teacher subject matter knowledge

The term "Teacher subject matter knowledge" is used nationally as well as globally. According to *Visible Learning*, it has a small effect size of only 0.10 (Figure 7.1).

When looking at the key figures, we note that three meta–analyses (1983, 2003 and 2007) were analyzed with a small confidence interval. This is interesting, as so much is claimed about the importance of subject knowledge which is not based on a large corpus of studies. Therefore, how are we to interpret this factor and how can the contradiction be resolved? A helpful principle appears to be the differentiation according to Lee

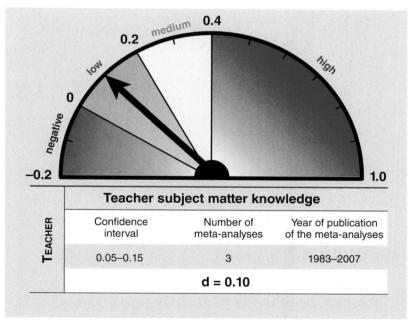

Teacher subject matter knowledge		
Confidence interval	Number of meta-analyses	Year of publication of the meta-analyses
0.05–0.15	3	1983–2007
d = 0.10		

FIGURE 7.1 Teacher subject matter knowledge

S. Shulman (1986), which divides a teacher's competence into at least three areas. First is subject matter knowledge. Second is educational competence. Third is didactic competence. While subject matter knowledge describes primarily the teacher's subject matter expertise and associated abilities in dealing with teaching content, the other two competence areas refer to non-subject matter aspects. But all three are referenced in the meta-analyses and the effects of each are low.

Educational competence mainly concerns the teacher's ability to establish contact and build a relationship with students, and to create an atmosphere of safety and trust. Didactic competence primarily describes the teacher's ability to prepare content in a comprehensible way, to explain facts clearly, to point out the essential aims, and – even more specifically – to be able to prepare clear and helpful board graphics and work sheets. If we start with this differentiation of a teacher's competence, the result from *Visible Learning* makes sense: We all know people who have incredible amounts of knowledge but are not able to pass that knowledge on – because they cannot express themselves clearly, because they are not approachable, and so on. The consequence is obvious: Subject matter knowledge by itself does not improve student achievement. It has to be combined with educational and didactic competence.

The important point is that it is not a matter of either-or. It is also not a matter of more-or-less. What counts is the combination of subject matter knowledge with educational and didactic competence. In this trinity, subject matter knowledge certainly occupies a prominent position – but only in this trinity. By itself and isolated from the other competence areas, subject matter knowledge can have no effect. If we reflect on first-phase teacher education at universities in this context, the following deficits become obvious: Subject matter content, didactics, and teaching skills, not to mention the interactions between them, are not taught properly. Little wonder that the factor "teacher education", meaning the initial training of teachers at universities, only has an effect size of 0.12.

Professional development

Becoming a teacher is one thing; being a teacher and remaining a teacher is another. This is why the professional development of teachers plays a major part in every country. Its effect size is relatively large at 0.49 and is based on a solid data pool (Figure 7.2). The details that

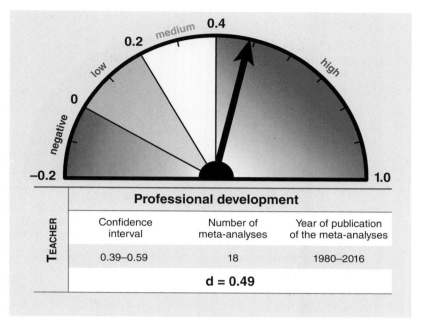

Professional development		
Confidence interval	Number of meta-analyses	Year of publication of the meta-analyses
0.39–0.59	18	1980–2016
d = 0.49		

(TEACHER)

FIGURE 7.2 Professional development

can be gleaned from the meta-analyses are interesting and already illustrated by the larger confidence interval. Teaching observations with subsequent discussions, for instance, are the most effective, whereas lectures, simulations, and preparing teaching materials are less helpful. In addition, a group composition of teachers from different types of schools is better than a group composition of teachers from the same type of school. All in all, then, this is an important area which can support teachers in all facets of their professional lives and have a lasting effect on student achievement.

Teacher–student relationships

The factor "Teacher–student relationships" has already been addressed: Classroom teaching by nature comprises a dialogue structure between learners and teachers who meet over the content of the lesson. The relationship is of central importance in this encounter. It is therefore not surprising that the effect size of the teacher–student relationship is very large, at 0.63 (Figure 7.3). One thing is still undisputed: An atmosphere of trust and confidence, of safety, caring, and goodwill, is indispensable for education in general and student achievement in

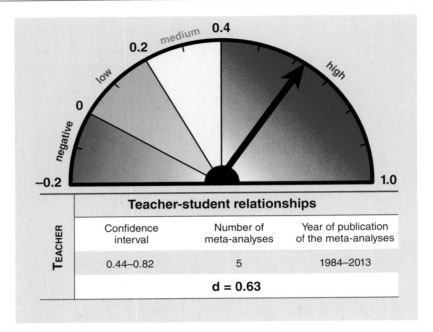

Teacher-student relationships		
Confidence interval	Number of meta-analyses	Year of publication of the meta-analyses
0.44–0.82	5	1984–2013
d = 0.63		

FIGURE 7.3 Teacher-student relationships

particular. In such an atmosphere, mistakes are not seen as deficits, but as an important step on the road to *Visible Learning* and successful teaching. This is precisely the result provided by a meta-analysis conducted in 2007, and which is quoted in *Visible Learning*. The consequence of this meta-analysis is that "student-centered" and "passionate" teachers are the most successful. Such teachers are not so much concerned with their own knowledge and abilities as with the student's. Learners become the starting and finishing point of the teaching. The student's success becomes the teacher's success. The dominant attitude is that classroom teaching is an interactive process where both sides need one another. A failure to learn is not chalked up (exclusively) to learners, but is seen as a joint failure that simultaneously offers the necessity and the opportunity to try again and to keep on trying.

Teacher clarity

Although this factor appears entirely unproblematic with regard to comprehensibility and transfer, a look at the data raises a number of questions. While in the first draft of *Visible Learning* only one meta-analysis was found (from 1990), the database today is broader and contains at least three meta-analyses. The result is clear and supports the importance of teacher clarity: It is one of the most influential factors (Figure 7.4).

If we peruse further literature on this factor, the core message becomes clear: Jere Brophy (1999), Andreas Helmke (2010), and Hilbert Meyer (2013) point out that successful learning depends on the clarity teachers have about the goals, the content, the methods, and the media.

Teacher clarity is about deliberate consideration and sharing of goals, content, methods, and media. It is not enough, for example, for teachers to glance at the curriculum and believe they are sure of their goals. This may be helpful for the case at hand, but it is not sufficient. Curricula list only general goals that must be transposed onto the class situation and specified. It is about knowing what success looks like for these students right now. We must remember that different goals have to be defined depending on the student's skill level. If we look back at the previously explained factor "cognitive levels", we will see that there are at least three skill levels of learners: beginner, advanced, and expert. Once teachers have established clarity in their own ideas of goals, content, methods, and media, they will be able to transport that clarity to the classroom.

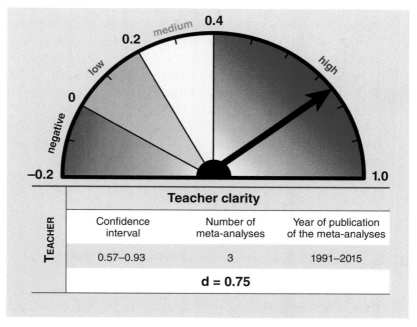

FIGURE 7.4 Teacher clarity

What core message can we infer from this for the teacher? The teacher determines the success or failure of learning. The classroom is a place of learning, not of structures and not of systems. It is the number one job of teachers to promote learning in all students. To do this, teachers must have a clear idea of what their students should be able to do at the end of the lessons and be able to express that idea in the form of goals. Teachers must present content to students in such a way that students can connect their prior knowledge and experience to it, and they must be able to build a deep relationship with learners. Passion is necessary – not only passion for the subject matter, but also for learners and the teaching profession to want to share this passion. We want to emphasize again that successful teachers are characterized by subject matter knowledge, educational competence, and didactic competence. The better these competences relate to one another, the greater their impact on learners.

But that is not all. Ultimately, all the knowledge and ability in the subject, in the pedagogy, and in the didactics are of little use if they are not supported by mindframes which place the learners and their education at the center. How teachers think, their mindframes, are therefore crucial. Mindframes show themselves in the way teachers think about what they do: What is the significance of errors in the learning process? Are they something to avoid? Or are they something that is part of learning, even necessary and welcome? Why is it worth asking learners what they think of the lessons? Is it because feedback from learners is the engine of their own teaching development? These or similar questions are intended to clarify what is meant when teacher professionalism is presented as a symbiosis of competence and attitude. In this respect, it is not only about the knowledge and ability of teachers, but also about their will and judgment (Figure 7.5).

Against this background, look again at the factor selection presented in Table 7.1 and consider: To what extent do the determined effect sizes fit the formulated core message (Table 7.2)?

CORE MESSAGE

The teacher's impact on the student's achievement level is enormous. It depends primarily on the mutual interactions between subject matter knowledge, pedagogical competence, and didactic competence – and the resulting passion with which teachers approach their students. Competences and attitudes are important. The mindframes of teachers are the center of expertise.

FIGURE 7.5 ACAC model

If we look at the core messages of the factors discussed in this chapter and try to collect them together, we can focus them as follows: How teachers think about their job matters. Two comments about that statement are necessary. First, the emphasis is on the plural. What are needed are not lone warriors, but cooperation between teachers and all those involved in the educational process. Teaching needs to become more of a shared profession – our peers should be critics of our thinking, of our expectations, and help us see our impact on our students. Second, not every teacher is automatically successful. Rather, a teacher must have particular attributes. We will return to both aspects in Chapter 8 in order to further sharpen the focus of the message.

TABLE 7.2

	NEGATIVE d<0	LOW 0<d<0.2	MEDIUM 0.2<d<0.4	HIGH d>0.4
Micro-teaching				1.01
Professional development				0.49
Student rating of quality of teaching				0.49
Teacher clarity				0.75
Teacher credibility				0.90
Teacher education		0.12		
Teacher effects			0.32	
Teacher estimates of achievement				1.41
Teacher expectations				0.57
Teacher performance pay				
Teacher personality			0.26	
Teacher subject matter knowledge		0.10		
Teacher verbal ability			0.22	
Teacher–student relationships				0.63
Teachers not labeling students				0.61
Teaching communication skills and strategies				0.43

Summary

■ **What is important in the domain "Teacher"?**

The domain "Teacher" describes attributes and characteristics of teachers, among them the factors "teacher clarity", "teacher–student relationships", and "teacher subject matter knowledge".

■ **What impact does teacher subject matter knowledge have on student achievement?**

Teacher subject matter knowledge by itself has virtually no impact on student achievement. It can become effective and be a central indicator only when combined with educational and didactic competence.

■ **What impact does professional development have on student achievement?**

Professional development has a profound impact on student achievement. However, this is not true of all kinds of professional development. The quality of the training is crucial.

■ **What impact does the teacher–student relationship have on student achievement?**

The teacher–student relationship has a huge impact on student achievement. Without a foundation of trust, learning and teaching are virtually impossible.

■ **What impact does teacher clarity have on student achievement?**

Teacher clarity has a huge impact on student achievement, since it guarantees that the teacher knows what successful learning looks like and can proceed accordingly. Just knowing the goals of the curriculum is not enough. It is more important to define different requirement levels according to the students' abilities.

■ **What core messages can we infer from this with regard to teachers?**

Teachers are one of the most important factors when it comes to student achievement. Subject matter knowledge alone is not enough. It must be accompanied by educational and didactic competence. Finally, the right mindframes are needed to bring knowledge, ability, will, and judgment into everyday school and teaching. Thus, the teacher's passion for the subject, for the students, and for the profession of teaching is crucial.

References

Brophy, J. E. (1999). Teaching (pp. 8–9). New York: International Academy of Education and the International Bureau of Education.

Helmke, A. (2010). Unterrichtsqualität und Lehrerprofessionalität. Diagnose, Evaluation und Verbesserung des Unterrichts. Stuttgart: Klett.

Meyer, H. L. (2013). Was ist guter Unterricht? (9. Edition). Berlin: Cornelsen Scriptor.

Shulman, L. S. (1986). Those who understand: Knowledge growth in teaching. *Educational Researcher*, 15(2), 4–14.

8

What are the landmarks? A summary

GOALS AND CONTENT

In this chapter, we will compare the impact of the nine domains. As a result, we will once again focus on the teacher and his or her role in the classroom. When you have read this chapter, you should be able to answer the following questions:

■ What comparative impacts do the nine domains have on student achievement?

■ What does this mean for the role of the teacher in the classroom?

■ What constitutes teacher expertise?

If we take the average effect sizes of the nine domains and compare them to one another, we create the pie chart shown in Figure 8.1.

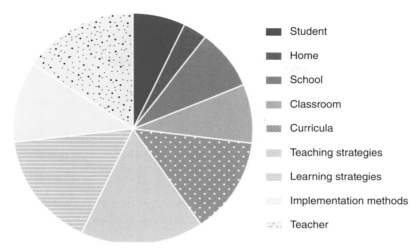

Student

Home

School

Classroom

Curricula

Teaching strategies

Learning strategies

Implementation methods

Teacher

FIGURE 8.1 Pie chart of the nine domains

We can draw two conclusions from this illustration. First, all domains contribute to student achievement. This is crucial, because it means that the responsibility does not rest on the shoulders of the few, such as teachers, but is borne by many. In addition, the domains all interact with one another. Cooperation on an equal footing among all levels and persons involved is therefore necessary, and any discussion about school and teaching alone runs the risk of being limiting if it focuses on only one area. This conclusion must be drawn when we consider the individual domains in light of the teacher's impact.

The domains "Student" and "Home" are colored dark blue because they have great impact but are not easily accessible to the teacher. For instance, parents' employment status is enormously important to student achievement, but teachers have no way of influencing these situations. The same goes for learners' natural aptitudes, where teachers also have little or no impact. Nevertheless, there are a number of factors that a teacher must know about in order to be able to teach successfully, for example, prior knowledge and experience.

The domains "School", "Classroom", and "Curricula" are depicted in blue, because teachers have some impact on the factors in these domains. Structures do not work in isolation but must be brought to life by those involved. Teachers thus have some impact on them; however, school administrators have the most impact.

The domains "Teaching strategies", "Implementation strategies", and "Learning strategies" are colored light blue and the domain

"Teacher" the lightest blue because they are particularly dependent on the teachers' competences and attitudes. Together, they represent the largest proportion of impacts on student achievement and can affect all the other domains.

Against this background it becomes clear that structures and framework conditions are important, but human interactions are decisive. Thus people bring structures to life. The comparison of factors in the domains of "School" and "Classroom" on the one hand and factors in the domains "Teaching strategies", "Implementation methods", and "Learning strategies" (summarized as "Teaching"), and "Teacher" on the other hand clarifies this idea (Table 8.1).

It follows, then, that teachers play a central role in student achievement, but this is not true of all teachers, only some. *Visible Learning* sparks a new debate regarding teachers with its results: The major findings point clearly to the important role of expertise. What constitutes expertise? An expert teacher is not necessarily the one with

TABLE 8.1

"SCHOOL" AND "CLASSROOM"		"TEACHING" AND "TEACHER"	
FACTOR	**d**	**FACTOR**	**d**
Finances	0.19	Feedback	0.70
School size	0.43	Goals	0.59
Principals/school leaders	0.28	Providing formative evaluation	0.53
Single-sex schools	0.08	Direct instruction	0.45
Summer vacation	−0.02	Cooperative learning	0.47
Ability grouping	0.11	Deliberate practice	0.49
Acceleration	0.58	Self-reported grades	1.22
Multi-grade/multi-age classes	0.04	Meta-cognitive strategies	0.52
Retention	−0.30	Teacher subject matter knowledge	0.09
Open vs. traditional	0.02	Teacher–student relationships	0.63
Class size	0.14	Teacher clarity	0.75
School calendars/ timetables	0.09	Teacher credibility	0.90
Overall effect	**0.14**	**Overall effect**	**0.61**

the deepest subject matter knowledge, but rather the one who is also able to hold a dialogue with learners, and to build a relationship with them and use these skills to then impact their learning.

The expert teacher must be able to translate his or her knowledge into the language of the students. By this we mean the interplay of subject matter knowledge, educational competence, and didactic competence. Howard Gardner and colleagues talk about the "Three Es": Excellence, Ethics, and Engagement (Gardner et al., 2001). The combination of the three Es is what constitutes expertise. In that sense, an expert teacher is not necessarily one who has enough years of teaching experience. Some currents in expert research assume that it takes ten years to become an expert teacher. That may be true in some cases, but this does mean teachers with this experience are necessarily experts: How many teachers are there who have been in the job for 20 or 30 years and who are still teaching at the level of novice educator? And how many teachers are there who prove that they are already an expert from their very first classroom lesson? In light of this fact, common evaluation practices that rank teachers depending on their years of service appear all but absurd.

It is not the number of years that makes the difference; nor is it the number of hours a teacher spends working in the job – according to the principle: the more, the better. This is another misconception in teaching practice that often makes life difficult for beginning teachers. It is the impact on the students. It is being clear and defending this notion of impact, it is high expectations, it is impacting all students, and it is much more than just achievement. It is imbuing students with a passion for learning, creating classrooms that make them want to come back and engage and invest in learning, it is (as John Hattie says so often in his more recent books) about the skill, will, and thrill of learning.

In consequence, expertise in the context of education lies in the fact that a teacher's actions are marked by caring, control, and clarity, that the teacher's classroom teaching offers challenges, sparks fascination, that the teacher listens to students' opinions and guides them towards solid knowledge. It can be shown, for example, that expert teachers pose much more appropriately challenging tasks that require students to apply their newly gained knowledge and transfer it to previously unknown situations, while non-experts often limit themselves to tasks where the newly learned knowledge only has to be repeated. Expertise in this sense is not a matter of years of service or work effort. It is about knowing how to set appropriately challenging success criteria, it is understanding where the students start, and it is about closing this gap between where they start and the criteria of success.

CORE MESSAGE

Teachers must be experts in teaching. Educational expertise becomes apparent when the teacher's actions are marked by caring, control, and clarity, when teaching offers challenges and sparks fascination, when the teacher listens to students' opinions and guides them towards solid knowledge. This is what we need to respect and invest in.

Passionate teachers are those who have the greatest impact on learners. Much more important than what we do is how and why we do it. We need teachers who do not see teaching as a monologue but as a dialogue, who keep searching for something within their students that nobody knows about and nobody believes in any longer, who can talk about their knowledge but also their lives with competence, who exchange ideas and get together with colleagues and who meet the students on an equal footing, knowing that they need the students as much as the students need them. Teachers thus fulfill a particular role in the classroom, which *Visible Learning* variously calls that of an activator, an evaluator, and at other times that of a change agent. A central prerequisite for this idea is a comparison from *Visible Learning* (Table 8.2).

The allocation of the individual factors can certainly be criticized and generate opposition. But the core message seems undisputable: The successful teacher acts as an activator. He or she always keeps

TABLE 8.2

TEACHER AS ACTIVATOR	d	TEACHER AS FACILITATOR	d
Feedback	0.70	Gaming/simulation	0.33
Reciprocal teaching	0.74	Inductive teaching	0.58
Meta-cognitive strategies	0.52	Inquiry-based teaching	0.41
Self-verbalization/self-questioning	0.62	Individualized instruction	0.23
Direct instruction	0.45	Web-based learning	0.16
Goals	0.59	Student control over learning	0.02
Teacher clarity	0.75	Discovery-based teaching	0.27
Goal difficulty	0.60	Open vs. traditional	0.02
Overall effect	**0.62**	**Overall effect**	**0.25**

an eye on the goals of the lesson, reviews the chosen methods, and takes the students' circumstances into account. A teacher as facilitator, on the other hand, works with more restraint and often leaves it to chance whether students learn anything and what they learn.

The decisive factor for a teacher as activator is evidence. The term "evidence" is used in an almost inflationary and often vague manner in current discourse. It spans everything from strict research design with trial and control groups to reflective self-observation, all the way to a combination of the two.

Visible Learning is associated more closely with this latter current — largely because it places central importance on empirical teacher self-help. "Know thy impact!" has become a mantra, meaning that the teacher questions the effect of his or her own actions and looks for empirical evidence of this impact. According to the results of *Visible Learning*, we can name the following factors. In light of the current data set, it proves to be particularly effective:

The learner should be seen as the starting point for education and classroom teaching — with all of his or her strengths and weaknesses. A teacher–student relationship based on cooperation and acceptance is indispensable, and one of the most important factors for successful teaching and visible learning ($d = 0.63$). Mistakes should not be ashamed of, but be seen as important information on the road to successful teaching. This makes one thing clear: Classroom instruction is not a one-way street, but an intensive dialogue between learner and teacher. Feedback is a central factor, because it is essential for communication in and about the teaching ($d = 0.70$), as is teacher clarity ($d = 0.75$), because it sets the standard for teaching and evaluation. Apart from this, it is undisputed that peers and the learning group play an important role ($d = 0.53$) — cooperative learning, for instance, is superior to competitive and individualistic learning ($d = 0.42$). Direct instruction ($d = 0.45$) is thus a consequence of what was said before — not misunderstood as frontal teaching, but as a teaching style that determines goals, content, methods, and media based on information about the students' ability level.

CORE MESSAGE

Teacher mindframes and evidence-based evaluation are crucial for the full impact of teaching. This results in the teacher's role being that of an activator.

So: The teacher's ways of thinking are what matter. One single teacher does not make the difference, but all those involved in the education process must work together and can be most successful when they take advantage of cooperation among learners, teachers, educators, parents, etc. This also shows that teachers are indeed important in the education process, but certainly not solely important. Nothing works without the learners, and their circumstances cannot be ignored. Another thought that needs to be emphasized in light of the increasingly politically driven "nationalization" of education is that nothing works without the parents. From an educational point of view, our international audience justly stipulates that the duty to educate children and adolescents falls first and foremost to the parents.

CORE MESSAGE

Student achievement is a complex field that requires cooperation at all levels and among all those involved. Nobody is solely responsible for everything.

In light of the above, it is obvious that *Visible Learning* is not about frontal teaching as a panacea, nor is it about teachers being all-knowing and omnipotent. And since teachers always consider themselves also to be learners, they are not lone warriors. Teachers need feedback too, and they also make the most progress when working in a group. Knowing that, it is a huge disappointment to find out that, over the course of a week, teachers talk to one another about anything but their own teaching! Back to the core business seems to be the only conclusion.

The grammar of learning

One of the most important results to emerge from *Visible Learning* are the following principles.

Successful learning requires:

- Commitment and effort
- Cooperation and exchange
- Detours and aberrations
- Positive relationships
- Errors

- Challenges instead of under- or overstrain,
- Intensive discussions and feedback
- A common vision of learning.

These principles for learning success describe the grammar of learning, because learning cannot take place without them. In this sense, they are the set of rules that teachers must observe and reflect on time and again in the planning, implementation, and evaluation of lessons. Incidentally, all the structural measures, however well-thought out, and all the revolutionary achievements of the digital age will not change this. The grammar of learning is a human law that follows (if at all) evolutionary changes, but certainly not social, industrial, or technical changes.

In view of this result, it is worth taking a look at a selection of factor bundles. With their help, the grammar of learning can be further specified and clarified by a number of factors. In this respect, it is not a question of presenting a comprehensive analysis, but of providing a further and relatively pointed illustration in light of the considerations that have been made.

"The drivers"

There is a bundle of factors within both the domains "Learner" and "Home" that make it clear how important it is to take the learner's initial learning situation into account. At the same time, these factors show which foundation learning success is based on and how this can be achieved in the family environment (Table 8.3).

"The preventers"

In a similar way to the bundle of factors "The drivers", factors can be identified in the domains "Student" and "Home" that not only make learning more difficult but may even prevent it. As a teacher, in view of the negative effects associated with this problem, it is always advisable to react when they first come to light. Once these factors are present, it becomes difficult to eliminate them. Prevention is better than intervention (Table 8.4).

"The purposeful"

Starting from the juxtaposition of the teacher as activator on the one hand and the teacher as moderator on the other, a bundle of factors

TABLE 8.3

Achieving motivation and approach	0.62
Concentration/persistence/engagement	0.42
Deep motivation and approach	0.71
Piagetian programs	1.28
Prior ability	0.82
Prior achievement	0.54
Relations of high school to university achievement	0.53
Self-concept	0.43
Self-efficacy	0.77
Working memory	0.67
Home environment	0.53
Parental involvement	0.42
Overall effect	**0.65**

TABLE 8.4

Anxiety	−0.37
ADHD	−0.90
Depression	−0.35
Boredom	−0.49
Corporal punishment in the home	−0.33
Television	−0.15
Overall effect	**−0.43**

that concentrates on the goals from various points of view comes into focus. It is striking that each of these factors is extremely important for learning success. From the teacher's point of view, it is therefore more worthwhile than ever to think about the goals, to disclose them, and to discuss them with the students. This creates the best conditions for the goals to set the challenge in the learning process (Table 8.5).

"The evergreens"

As large as the number of methods and media has become and as numerous as the studies on them are, there is a bundle of factors that can claim for itself, irrespective of their age, the learners' performance level, the

subject, and the type of school. In this sense, they are didactic–methodical evergreens! Although there are pitfalls associated with each of these
factors, the potential is enormous, and it is recommended that they be
exploited collectively and in exchange with learners (Table 8.6).

TABLE 8.5

Goal commitment	0.44
Goal difficulty	0.60
Goal intentions	0.41
Goals	0.59
Teacher clarity	0.79
Direct instruction	0.45
Overall effect	**0.54**

TABLE 8.6

Classroom discussion	0.82
Cognitive task analysis	1.09
Feedback	0.70
Goals	0.59
Peer tutoring	0.66
Planning and prediction	0.56
Providing formative evaluation by teachers	0.53
Questioning	0.46
Worked examples	0.47
Deliberate practice	0.49
Meta-cognitive strategies	0.52
Mnemonics	0.78
Practice testing	0.51
Rehearsal and memorization	0.57
Self-regulation strategies	0.45
Time on task	0.50
Cooperative learning	0.47
Cooperative vs. competitive learning	0.58
Cooperative vs. individualistic learning	0.62
Direct instruction	0.45
Overall effect	**0.60**

"The challengers"

In addition to "the evergreens" set of factors, there are a number of factors that have a lot of potential – but this is not independent of the age of the learners and their performance level. Rather, it is precisely these questions that need to be answered first in order to decide whether these factors are being used at the right time. If this fit is successful, they help set the challenge in the learning process. They make learning neither too easy nor too difficult (Table 8.7).

"The dialogic"

Teaching is an encounter between individuals. This philosophical reflection finds convincing empirical confirmation. Several factors point to the need to see teaching as an interaction between people, as dialogue. The better this succeeds, the more effective the teaching processes become (Table 8.8).

"The confidence builders"

Another philosophical position is that teaching is essentially a relationship, and it is therefore worth investing time in the relationship for it to work. A bundle of factors confirms this forcefully. Learning needs trust and confidence. Learning needs security. Learning needs a positive error culture. Competence and attitude on the part of the teacher is decisive for this to be successful (Table 8.9).

TABLE 8.7

Concept mapping	0.61
Student control over learning	0.02
Record keeping	0.51
Self-verbalization/self-questioning	0.62
Discovery-based teaching	0.27
Homework	0.32
Inductive teaching	0.58
Inquiry-based teaching	0.41
Jigsaw method	1.20
Problem-based learning	0.33
Mobile phones	0.39
Overall effect	**0.48**

TABLE 8.8

Cooperative learning	0.47
Cooperative vs. competitive learning	0.58
Cooperative vs. individualistic learning	0.62
Direct instruction	0.45
Interactive video methods	0.52
Jigsaw method	1.20
Philosophy in schools	0.43
Reciprocal teaching	0.74
Questioning	0.46
Classroom behavior	0.60
Classroom cohesion	0.53
Peer influences	0.53
Scaffolding	0.96
Small group learning	0.45
Overall effect	**0.61**

TABLE 8.9

Student rating of quality of teaching	0.49
Teacher clarity	0.75
Teacher credibility	0.90
Teacher estimates of achievement	1.42
Teacher expectations	0.57
Teacher–student relationships	0.63
Teachers not labeling students	0.61
Teaching communication skills and strategies	0.43
Overall effect	**0.73**

"The self-regulators"

The extension of the data set to over 1,400 meta–analyses revealed a bundle of factors that appeared in the first edition of *Visible Learning*: Learners must see themselves as their own teachers. A multitude of factors underpins this focus (Table 8.10).

August Hermann Niemeyer was one of the founding fathers of German educational science in the eighteenth century. His motto for education and teaching was: "I no longer need you!" Maria Montessori expressed her core ideas in a similar thought early in the

TABLE 8.10

Deliberate practice	0.49
Effort management	0.77
Elaboration and organization	0.75
Evaluation and reflection	0.75
Help seeking	0.66
Imagery	0.45
Meta-cognitive strategies	0.52
Mnemonics	0.78
Note taking	0.41
Outlining and transforming	0.75
Record keeping	0.51
Rehearsal and memorization	0.57
Self-regulation strategies	0.45
Self-reported grade	1.22
Self-verbalization/self-questioning	0.62
Strategy monitoring	0.54
Strategy to integrate with prior knowledge	0.93
Study skills	0.46
Summarization	0.90
Transfer strategies	0.75
Underlining and highlighting	0.50
Overall effect	**0.65**

twentieth century: "Help me to do it myself!" And *Visible Learning for Teachers* states: "The teacher has the skill to 'get out of the way' when learning is progressing towards the success criteria", and that one aim of schooling is to "make the student their own teacher".

Successful teachers then enter the classroom with the attitude of an activator who guides his or her class responsibly and humanely. Successful teachers also do not approach their class from a position of authority as one who decides everything and sets the tone, but guide their students gently and empathetically towards their success criteria in a constant exchange about goals, content, methods, and media. They exchange ideas with colleagues about the right ways, round-about ways, and wrong ways, cooperate with parents and, together with their students, approach the goal, step by step – but every learner has to master for him- or herself that very last step.

Summary

- **What comparative impact do the six domains "Student", "Home environment", "School", "Curricula", "Teaching", and "Teacher" have on student achievement?**

Each of these six domains has some impact on learning success and must be given consideration. Still, the teacher occupies a prominent position, because this is *the* central role in the classroom as a place of education.

- **What does this mean for the role of the teacher in the classroom?**

Teachers have the largest impact on student achievement when they act as activators. They are aware of the goals, content, methods, and media, and select them according to student feedback. Based on an intensive student–teacher relationship, they use feedback to evaluate not only the result but also the process of learning. This enables them to make the necessary changes to their teaching habits.

- **What constitutes teacher expertise?**

Expertise is not the same as experience. Rather, it is made up of subject matter knowledge, educational competence, and didactic competence, in addition to a strong interconnectedness among these areas. This emphasizes the attitudes with which teachers approach their teaching and meet their students.

Reference

Gardner, H., Csíkszentmihályi, M., & Damon, W. (2001). Good work: When excellence and ethics meet. New York: Basic Books.

9

What's missing:
An outlook

REFLECTIVE TASK

Reflect on what you have read so far and ask the question: What is a "good" school? Can you give a comprehensive answer to this question with the help of the core messages of *Visible Learning*, or are there limits you face in the course of your everyday teaching?

GOALS AND CONTENT

This chapter addresses the limitations of *Visible Learning*. To do so, we will introduce Ken Wilber's epistemological quadrant model and apply it to the educational context. When you have read this chapter, you should be able to answer the following questions:

- What perspectives of a complex phenomenon does Wilber highlight?
- What is the risk of abridgement when considering these perspectives?
- What are the limitations of *Visible Learning*?
- What makes a "good" school?

Visible Learning has changed the debate about teaching and learning and the way we think about classroom teaching. It is certainly important, but it will not be the last book to be written about teaching, not least because it is subject to limitations. This is not a criticism, but applies to all books.

To explain these limitations in more detail, we will use Ken Wilber's epistemological model. Ken Wilber is currently one of the most translated thinkers in the world. He has developed a theory based on the work of Karl Popper and Jürgen Habermas. His core statement is that complex phenomena may be viewed from four different perspectives, and that each of these perspectives is important. Accordingly, he considers it problematic when a problem is argued from only one perspective. Essentially, Wilber differentiates four approaches and arranges them according to the model presented in Figure 9.1, which is why he calls it a quadrant model. The following first explains the model according to Wilber before applying it to *Visible Learning*.

Wilber defines an objective approach. It is dominated by empirical methods and insight is gained through measurement, testing, and so on. An example of a statement in this quadrant would be: "It's raining outside." Anybody can verify this statement quickly and easily. It is clear, then, that statements in the objective quadrant claim to be true.

This differs from the subjective approach which is mainly about needs, interests, and feelings. An example would be the answer "I'm fine" to the question "How are you?" It is obvious that the truth of this statement cannot be empirically verified: We cannot use measurement or tests to check whether someone is telling the truth or

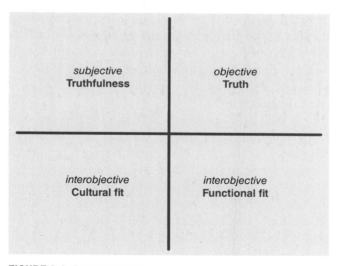

FIGURE 9.1 Four approaches

lying. We can try to gain additional information by observing gestures and facial expressions, but at the end of the day we have to settle for the level of interpretation. We can only try to read and understand the truthfulness of a statement, but we can never be completely sure of our interpretation. Consequently, Wilber states that statements in the subjective quadrant do not claim to be objective truth but subjective truthfulness.

Furthermore, Wilber defines an intersubjective approach. This approach focuses on the relationships between people. Values, norms, rules, and rituals play a major part and impact the way people think and act. They cannot be empirically determined or set by the individual. Rather, they need debate and discourse. Statements in the intersubjective quadrant therefore claim neither truth nor truthfulness. Ken Wilber calls it a "cultural fit". We can illustrate this point by imagining a situation where a person who has never been exposed to soccer decides to watch a soccer game at a stadium. This person would be utterly overwhelmed and would not be able to understand anything that is happening. He would be lacking the cultural knowledge to fit the situation.

Finally, Wilber talks about an interobjective approach. This addresses systemic connections: No one person exists by themselves, but we are all integrated into different contexts – in families, the economy, politics, our church, to name but a few of the most important examples. According to Niklas Luhmann's system theory, which may be associated with this quadrant, there are numerous tensions between the individual systems. These are primarily due to the different codes with which the systems are expressed and how they work. Politics is mainly about power, economics is about profits, church is about belief, etc. These different interests can lead to conflicts and controversy. Resolving these conflicts requires statements that claim to be a functional fit.

If we look at a complex phenomenon in light of the quadrant model, it is plain to see that we need to differentiate among at least four perspectives. Each of these perspectives is important and cannot be replaced by another. Wilber points out that the risk is therefore inherent in abridged arguments from only one perspective, as this will always lead to false assumptions and false conclusions.

If we apply this quadrant model to the question "What makes a 'good' school?", which is at the center of *Visible Learning*, we can name four sub-questions that at the same time illustrate the limitations of *Visible Learning*.

What is an "effective" school?

When we talk about measuring and testing in the educational context, effectiveness is the defining criterion. Prime examples are international comparative studies like PISA and others, where the effectiveness of education systems in different countries is compared by means of measuring mathematical, scientific, and linguistic competence.

These abilities are also the basis for many of the more than 80,000 quantitative empirical studies used in the 1,400 meta-analyses in *Visible Learning*. This establishes a particular focus regarding the term "education" in general and student achievement in particular. *Visible Learning* may be considered one of the largest source of empirical educational research available today covering achievement effects. It is a veritable treasure chest of thoughts about the effectiveness of learning and teaching. However, education and student achievement are not limited to the competences mentioned above.

Let us remember at this point Howard Gardner's "multiple intelligences". There are also motoric, social, affective, moral, ethical, and religious competences that are also part of the responsibility of education and teaching but are barely or never taken into account in *Visible Learning*. From the beginning, it has continually claimed that achievement is only one (yes, important) outcome of schooling. There is no question that these other competences are less important. The reason is that there have been far fewer quantitative-empirical studies of these competences – there are teams working on projects to synthesize outcomes relating to motivation, effectiveness, special education students, higher education, entrepreneurship, and creativity, and there is an exciting new development in synthesizing qualitative research. These will add much to the debate.

What is a "joyful" school?

The limitation to a selection of certain competences must also be considered in another context. Education is not made up only of competences, and school is not limited to being as effective as possible. The interests, desires, and needs of all those involved are just as important. The experience "in the now" of being a child is imperative. We can illustrate this point by looking at one of the PISA winners: China has one of the most effective education systems in the world. Chinese students are among the best with regard to mathematical, scientific, and linguistic competence.

This is not surprising when one looks at Chinese schools. These students cram. Breadth of knowledge is valued, and success at exams reflects pride in family and country. It has little to do with classroom teaching as we know it. Teaching in Chinese schools rather resembles high-level drill. There is no communication in the classroom, no interaction among the people involved, and no passion on either side. There is collusion in this cramming and exam success with parents and across most aspects of society. Resilience, grit, and self-motivation are regarded as valuable assets – not surprising in a communist country, but some of its people are not yet ready for a communist society. This kind of teaching may be effective in sorting out the employment lines from schools, feeding the desires of parents in a competitive society, and leading to better exam results, but if introduced into Europe it would not necessarily be perceived as pleasureable or fulfilling. We all know that effective time is not necessarily always fulfilling, and conversely fulfilling time is not always used effectively. But education requires both. That the perspective of pleasure is usually left out of the discussion has to do with an overemphasis on effectiveness. In the end, this can lead to an optimization trap, as Julian Nida-Rümelin points out in a different context. If we look at *Visible Learning* from this vantage point, we will see that the question about a "joyful" school is only touched upon in the over 250 factors. However, this limitation is pointed out in *Visible Learning* and there are many comments about how passion in teaching can be infectious, that there is real pleasure in learning to learn, and that experiencing joy and fairness is key to building trust and relationships.

What is a "culturally fitting" school?

When we consider the question of cultural fit in the context of education, we mean questions of goals and content about what is taught in schools. These cannot be determined empirically, nor can they be defined by the individual. The question of what should be learned in school and why must be answered through debate and discourse. Every culture has to ask itself these questions. The term "education", then, has to be continuously redefined as well. What is considered important today may be obsolete tomorrow. Let us think about environmental education, for example, which became particularly pressing with the nuclear disaster in Chernobyl in 1986, or the issue of inclusion, which currently dominates a lot of discussion about education and teaching. These issues were hardly pressing 40 years ago;

we continually create hard debates about the purpose of schooling in our society today.

It is therefore obvious that the question about "culturally fitting" schools is not and cannot be answered in *Visible Learning*. However, we can see how important it is by giving an example. A few years ago in the western states of Germany enormous efforts were made to track the "Gymnasium", a school which prepares pupils for university entrance. Many made only structural adjustments, and what was once taught in nine years was compressed into eight – without sufficient deliberation about what content should be adjusted or removed. The consequences quickly became apparent: Overwhelmed students, overburdened teachers, and irritated parents. Although improvements have been initiated in most cases there was a step back to nine years. Thus the reform of the German "Gymnasium" may be seen as an example of the importance of a "culturally fitting" school.

What is a "functionally fitting" school?

The significance of this question is again best explained using an example: The German "Hauptschule", a lower track secondary school, has been abolished in many areas. What was the problem with the Hauptschule? Certainly not that it was ineffective. We know from a number of studies that some Hauptschule students achieved as highly as their peers attending "Realschule" (higher tracked secondary school), and some even achieved at the same level as students attending the Gymnasium (highest tracked secondary school). So that was not the problem. The Hauptschule was an "effective" school. The problem also was not that students did not like to go to Hauptschule. They enjoyed their school years just as much as students at the other types of schools. Thus the Hauptschule was also a "joyful" school. And due to the heterogeneity of its students, Hauptschule was also a "culturally fitting" school. The variety of cultures and the different family contexts which students brought to Hauptschule required many different forms of education in daily classroom teaching: Intercultural education, environmental education, media education, successful violence prevention, etc. The Hauptschule therefore faced considerable challenges with regard to its cultural fit. The problem with the Hauptschule lies in the interobjective quadrant: If a type of school does not succeed in guiding its graduates into the working world and giving them opportunities to find their place in life because, for instance, companies would rather hire (less well-qualified) students with Realschule or Gymnasium backgrounds, then it no longer has any justification.

A school that prepares young people for unemployment should rightly be abolished. Hauptschule, as shown in the discussion above, lacked primarily the "functional fit". Whether simply relabeling the schools, as is currently being practiced in several German states, will be enough to save this type of school is doubtful. Systemic problems cannot be solved by changing a name. They need systemic solutions. If we apply these thoughts to *Visible Learning*, we will see that the research does not cover this issue. The question of a "functionally fitting" school is a culture-specific question which every nation has to answer for itself and one that cannot be answered by a synthesis of meta-analyses.

These examples illustrate the core idea which Ken Wilber pursues with his quadrant model. Complex phenomena cannot be addressed from only one perspective. Rather, we must argue from multiple perspectives. The same applies to *Visible Learning*, which does not cover all of the quadrants. It certainly does yield important results for discussing a sustainable education system. However, *Visible Learning* does not completely illuminate the necessary discussion but includes certain focal points. It should therefore be supplemented with other approaches and additional work. The question of what makes a "good" school may subsequently be answered by addressing the sub-questions about "effective", "joyful", "culturally fitting", and "functionally fitting" schools and placing them in relation to one another (Figure 9.2).

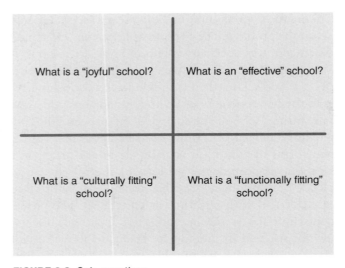

FIGURE 9.2 Sub-questions

Visible Learning is not the holy grail of classroom teaching, nor has it ended the search — and nor has it ever claimed this. Indeed, any such search is not very promising, because it presupposes that the holy grail of classroom teaching can be found — with two false consequences. First, if this were true, everybody would be able to learn everything. Second, everybody would be able to teach. Both are not the case. Instead, *Visible Learning* explains that the search for the holy grail of teaching must be aborted and we must set out in a different direction. Learning has been, is, and will remain strenuous, requires commitment, challenges, and mistakes, a positive relationship, appreciation, and a common vision of progress and learning. Likewise, teaching was, is, and remains a complex and demanding activity, the success of which cannot be readily programmed. It is these mind-frames towards learning and teaching that, over and above the many meta-analyses, bring the core idea of *Visible Learning* to the fore.

Summary

- **What perspectives of a complex phenomenon does Wilber differentiate?**

  Ken Wilber differentiates four approaches to reality. First, the objective approach, which is concerned with measuring and testing, and accordingly with truth. Second, the subjective approach, which is about wishes, interests, and needs, and therefore about truthfulness. Third, the intersubjective approach, which focuses on rituals, values, and norms, and emphasizes cultural fit. Fourth, the interobjective approach, which takes a systematic view and concentrates on the tensions between family, school, politics, economy, church, etc.

- **What is the risk of abridgement in light of these perspectives?**

  If we look at complex phenomena from only one perspective, we run the risk of overlooking important aspects and using limited arguments. It is therefore important to take all perspectives into account and relate them to one another.

- **What are the limitations of *Visible Learning*?**

  Because of its meta-analytical process, *Visible Learning* mainly argues in the objective quadrant and under the paradigm of measuring and testing. This leads to a certain limitation of the discussion. In addition, it focuses mainly on mathematical, scientific, and linguistic competence, which poses another limitation.

■ What makes a "good" school?

A "good" school cannot be defined solely by its effectiveness. It is just as important that school is perceived as fulfilling time, that school satisfies cultural responsibilities, and that it is functionally fitting from a systemic point of view. It is apparent that these perspectives have reciprocal effects on one another.

10

To start with: Ideas for practice

After looking at the results from *Visible Learning*, many teachers say: "Nobody can do this!" or: "We are burdened with so many things, sometimes overwhelmed, so all these suggestions are certainly well meant, but just not feasible."

This is not true. In fact, the results from *Visible Learning* show that about 50 percent of teachers are already doing everything *Visible Learning* suggests. In these cases, *Visible Learning* merely provides evidence for this to continue. It also acknowledges that the *Visible Learning* message can be introduced given that these successful teachers work in the same schools, with the same curricula, tests, and pressures, with the same school leaders, and often with the same students from the same families. Surely our aim is to upscale and train more teachers where all students are gaining more than a year's growth for a year's input.

So, what are these teachers doing differently? And how can the improvement work for everyone?

It is not productive to claim that teachers are not doing enough. Instead, we need to ask whether they always have the desired impact. *Visible Learning* offers important help with this inquiry by providing core messages that can shake up and question our own classroom teaching and actions. The most important core message in this context is this: See mistakes as opportunities and dare to make a change. This includes reflecting on existing practices. If these practices turn out to be ineffective in that they are not sufficiently enhancing student learning and encouraging students to invest in their learning, they should be abandoned. This frees up capacity and offers opportunities to initiate change. New and possibly more effective practices can be tested, implemented, and established.

The following is an example to illustrate these considerations (cf. Hattie & Zierer, 2018).

Kambrya College: Developing a common vision of school, teaching, and learning

In 2015, a multi-part documentary aired across Australia called *Revolution School*. This series was about a school development process and made major headlines. Kambrya College set out to turn itself from one of the worst schools in Australia to one of the best. Founded in 2002 in Berwick, an easternmost suburb about 50 kilometers from Melbourne central, the school now has more than 1,000 students, of which over 25 percent have a migration background and represent more than 35 nationalities – a typical school in the twenty-first century. In 2008, the school was flagged as a "red school" (i.e., low achievement and slow progress). So the school management team, headed by principal Michael Muscat, set out to contact and learn from, among others, the Graduate School of the University of Melbourne. During this exchange, numerous strategies were developed and procedures implemented to help the school progress. After a short time, the school underwent a transformation which led to its success. This success was nearly all due to the leadership team and the dedication and passion of the teachers. They used the research, they implemented and refined, and they relentlessly evaluated their impact. They did not hire consultants, not one of us ever set foot in the school; they had the forethought and mission to listen, learn, interpret, and do it themselves. They decided that the major focus would be on not asking about the best ways to teach but to continually interview the students about the best ways they wanted to learn. They learned a great deal about what it was like to be a student at Kambrya – and this led to the revolution; that is, the teachers focused on their impact, looking at their teaching through the eyes of their students. Against the background of these considerations, one of the many interventions has been selected as a first step on the road to implementing "*Visible Learning*" in practice.

In an intensive exchange process, the teaching staff agreed to make central factors of successful teaching with the help of visible word cards in the classroom and to focus on them again and again. The decision was made to focus on the factors "goals" and "success criteria". Of course, one could also name other factors (which they later adopted, such as "feedback", "challenge", "we welcome errors"). What was much more important, however, was, first, the underlying process whereby the staff collectively discussed learning success and teaching quality from the students' perspective; and second, the agreement to make this understanding the principle of all instruction. Classroom quality was thus visible not only to the teachers, but also and above all to the learners. The goal that the school has set for itself is not an easy one, but it is a lesson in evidence orientation: no more lessons in which the students are not clear why they are learning something. No more lessons in which the students are not shown what the success criteria are, and no more lessons in which students do not know what media they are using and for what purpose.

Ultimately, this communication process and the resulting understanding of teaching provided a guarantee for the success of Kambrya College. The college went from the bottom 10 percent in the state to the top 20 percent. Collective expectations of effectiveness and efficiency led to profound changes. We see in this process and in the agreement on the described instrument an evidence-based path that is worth taking.

So talk to your colleagues, and talk to your students about what it means to be a learner in this school. Define questions of teaching that become binding for you and visible to learners. Place these questions as a central focus in the classroom and refer to them again and again in class. Make learning visible, create challenges, and enable self-commitment, trust, appropriate expectations, and conceptual understanding.

The "Visible Learning Wheel": Six steps to success

To effect this change, let us recall two core messages from *Visible Learning*. First, the teacher's mindframes are one of the most important factors for Visible Learning and successful learning. It is less what we do and who we are, and more how we think, evaluate, and make decisions. Every teacher has to work on this. Second, evidence-based evaluation that examines the effects of teachers' actions and looks for empirical evidence is indispensable. This does not necessarily mean more tests as part of school inspection, PISA studies, etc. On the contrary, it is about quality interpretations: What data are available to me and how do I interpret those data to evaluate and make decisions about my actions and my role as a teacher? These are crucial questions. In this respect, we plainly reject the mere collection of data which are then laid to rest in data graveyards without being used for any further purpose.

The following overview, which we call the "Visible Learning Wheel" following Kambrya College, can provide additional support. Starting from the results of *Visible Learning*, we have taken up the idea of visualizing quality criteria of teaching and developed the Visible Learning Wheel (Figure 10.1). It includes the following factors, all of which are especially effective in the learning progress and learning success of students (cf. Hattie & Zierer, 2018):

- The factor "goal" or success criterion is one of the most effective factors, with an effect size of 0.59. It is not only important that teachers have this clarity; it is also crucial to show the students what they will learn and when the goal is achieved. As a result, the objectives are

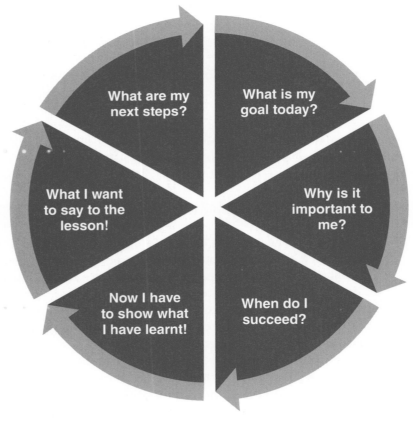

FIGURE 10.1 Visible Learning Wheel

always linked to the criterion for success. From the learners' point of view, this leads to questions for the Visible Learning Wheel, such as "What is my goal today?" and "When do I succeed?"

■ Learning cannot have a lasting effect without motivation. In this respect, the question "Why is it important to me?" addresses a key point of teaching. If teachers are able to give convincing answers and tie it into what the students have learned already, then students will be more successful. The factor "deep motivation and approach", with an effect size in the desired range of 0.71 in *Visible Learning*, supports this claim. For the Visible Learning Wheel the question that arises from the viewpoint of the learners is "Why is it important to me?"

■ The factor "formative evaluation" – back to the teacher – with an effect size of 0.53 shows how important and effective it is to bring learners back into situations where they have to show what they have learned and for teachers to listen to the outcome and adjust their teaching accordingly. The learner's performance with regard to the defined objectives of the lesson not only shows the learners where they are, but also, and above all, the teachers. Teachers need to seek feedback about their impact: What are the objectives? What content was understood? Who understood what? Which methods could be used in the long term? Which media are retrospectively effective? And was there sufficient improvement? The challenge "Now I have to show what I have learnt!" is therefore another building block of the Visible Learning Wheel.

■ A common thread throughout *Visible Learning* is that teachers must be seen as evaluators of their impact. Teachers must be aware of their impact. The factor "feedback", with an effect size of 0.70, reinforces this point. Two key aspects of successful feedback are pointed out. First, successful feedback is not a one-way street but a dialogue. In this respect, not only is the feedback from the teacher to the learners important; so is the feedback from the learners to the teacher. Second, feedback is not equal feedback. It proves particularly effective as long as there is information about the further learning process from the perspective of the students. For the Visible Learning Wheel these are the elements "What I want to say to the lesson" and "What are my next steps?"

It is necessary to offer one comment at this point to avoid misunderstandings: The Visible Learning Wheel is not to be viewed as restrictive, but as an expression of collective professionalization, and therefore a fundamental attitude of the teaching staff. For learners, it also leads to a visualization of learning and teaching. In this respect, it allows scope both in the intensity of use and in the sequence of its components. But there is no room for maneuver in the question of whether it is taken up again and again in class. Caution is therefore also called for: The Visible Learning Wheel is more than just a medium. It requires a deep understanding from and accordingly competence and attitude of teachers. Therefore it is not only important to know what and how to use it; it is also crucial to know why it is used.

In *10 Mindframes for Visible Learning*, we tackled the challenge of inferring practical recommendations from *Visible Learning*. The following ten mindframes are central:

1 I am an evaluator of my impact on student learning.

2 I see assessment as informing my impact and next steps.

3 I collaborate with my peers and my students about my concepts of progress and my impact.

4 I am a change agent and believe all students can improve.

5 I strive for challenge and not merely "doing your best".

6 I offer and help students understand feedback and I interpret and act on feedback given to me.

7 I engage as much in dialogue as in monologue.

8 I explicitly inform students what a successful impact looks like from the outset.

9 I build relationships and trust so that learning can occur in a place where it is safe to make mistakes and learn from others.

10 I focus on learning and the language of learning.

These ten mindframes serve to illustrate the crucial steps to make learning visible.

1. Mindframe: I am an evaluator of my impact on student learning

Educational expertise is shown by how teachers think about what they do. One of the most crucial questions is whether teachers want to know about their impact and make it visible. Teachers who have set themselves this goal and are consistently trying to implement it are fundamentally different from teachers who do not ask themselves this question. When you walk into a classroom and say to yourself, "My job here is to evaluate my impact", then students are the major beneficiaries. Getting into this mindframe the idea that "Teachers are to DIIE for!" is helpful: accurate **diagnosis**, appropriate **interventions**, quality **implementation**, and excellent **evaluation** of the interventions are the main steps of successful teaching.

2. Mindframe: I see assessment as informing my impact and next steps

In *Visible Learning* it was pointed out repeatedly that feedback in classroom teaching is not a one-way street but works both ways: From teacher to learners, which is discussed most often, but also from learners to teacher. The latter is indispensable for *Visible Learning*: Did the learners achieve their goals? And did they understand all of the lesson content? Which students made sufficient progress and which did not? It is only when teachers have this information that they can plan the next lesson. A contemplative look at learners' notebooks may sometimes be enough, and a critical look at grades is important for both students and teacher. In fact, these examinations provide important information about the teacher's success.

If a teacher does not have this information, he or she runs the risk of teaching above the learners' heads and leaving it up to chance whether the planning is suitable for the learners.

We have already mentioned that a teacher's own evaluation of the process and success of classroom teaching is not sufficient: Students have to learn to function in class and also evaluate their success. Students need to be actively engaged, but too many may appear to be concentrating, even if their hearts and minds are not in it. The reason is simple: It's how they avoid sanctions. In light of that fact, a classroom lesson may be rolling along perfectly from the teacher's point of view, but the students may be bored.

There are a number of assessment methods described in education literature – all have advantages and disadvantages. A process that does not involve high costs or much effort is a quiz or an exit test. Easy to handle, it delivers information about learning efficiently, and will thus reflect the impact of the teacher. So, integrate quizzes at the end of the lesson to help make learning visible. Figure 10.2 shows a worksheet from a lesson in which various deciduous trees were introduced on

1)					A	C	O	R	N	
2)				A	L	D	E	R		
3)					L	I	M	E		
4)			B	I	R	C	H			
5)				W	I	L	L	O	W	
6)			M	A	G	N	O	L	I	A
7)	B	E	E	C	H					
8)			N	U	T					

FIGURE 10.2 Quiz: Most important terms of the lesson

the basis of their leaves and fruits. If the learner has reached the success critierion he or she will be able to find the solution "all right".

3. Mindframe: I collaborate with my peers and my students about my concepts of progress and my impact

Cooperation among teaching staff appears indispensable for everything we have said thus far. Success is achieved only when teachers work together. Teachers are also learners, and as a rule they learn better together than they do alone: Teams can talk about and discuss the planning, execution, and evaluation of classroom teaching. In a team, strengths can be pooled and weaknesses compensated. In a team, responsibility can be shared. Teams can save time by dividing the work. In a team, one can share success and overcome failure. Most importantly, collaboration among peers assists in critiquing and clarifying our concepts of "impact", questions whether sufficient progress is being made, queries our notions of evidence, and helps evaluate the impact we are having on our students.

Try planning a lesson together. For example, use a placemat to clarify the different objectives and find a common denominator; the ideas of the different colleagues are on the sides and the agreement is noted in the middle (Figure 10.3).

Of course, not everyone always works well with everyone else and conflict is a possibility in any team. There is a strong need for social sensitivity, permitting turn taking so that others can express their views in order to make any group successful. But this justifies none of the preconceptions we often meet among teaching staff. One important instrument is team meetings which are similar to successful teaching in that they are characterized by clarity in terms

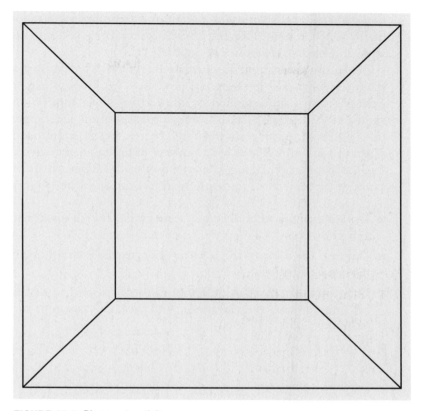

FIGURE 10.3 Placemat activity

of goals, content, methods, and media. And an insight into the effectiveness of cooperation is important, as Simon Sinek (2009) puts it: "Successful cooperation does not mean working together. Successful cooperation means trusting each other."

4. Mindframe: I am a change agent and believe all students can improve

Again, let us remember that the goal of *Visible Learning* is not to settle ongoing and long-standing method debates. Its purpose lies elsewhere. First, it is concerned with teachers' ability to evaluate the effects of their own teaching practices. Many kinds of empirical data are useful for developing this skill. Second, it is crucial to know that if classroom teaching proves to be ineffective, it is not all due to the learners. Teachers must also question their role and change their methods accordingly. This emphasizes the teacher's ability to apply a wide and flexible repertoire of methods.

Let us use an example to illustrate this point. Motivation is absolutely essential for the learning process – in *Visible Learning*, for example, this is underpinned by the factors "deep motivation and approach" ($d = 0.71$) and "achieving motivation and approach" ($d = 0.62$). Motivation should thus receive special attention in the classroom situation. There are a number of different strategies focusing, for instance, on factors like attention to the subject matter, relevance of the subject matter, learner satisfaction, or learner confidence:

- Use an example that does not seem to illustrate a given concept (attention).
- Connect the topic to the learners' everyday lives and show its significance (relevance).
- Offer different levels of difficulty in the classroom so that learners can approach the classroom with the expectation to succeed (confidence).
- Emphasize the learning success and progress that emerged during recent lessons (satisfaction).

The success of different methods depends substantially on their suitability for the various cognitive levels ("Piagetian programs", $d = 1.28$). This results in a teaching style that tries to achieve the highest possible level in terms of goals and is therefore challenging. In this context, the "1+" strategy was recognized in *Visible Learning*.

5. Mindframe: I strive for challenge and not merely "doing your best"

It is probably one of the most surprising findings of research into teachers' planning practices that many teachers barely think about goals. This fact is often assessed in very different ways: In experienced teachers, a lack of consideration of goals is seen to be less problematic and explained by the fact that they have taught the same lesson repeatedly. However, regardless of whether or not they have taught a lesson repeatedly, they have not taught it to the same learners.

By contrast, a lack of consideration of goals is severely criticized in beginning teachers, because without an awareness of the goals of the lesson, they cannot reflect on the success of their own teaching practices, which is however part of professional conduct. Just as importantly, they should share their goals or success criteria with their students.

In this context, it is undisputed that teacher clarity (d = 0.75) with regard to goals (d = 0.59) is one of the most important factors of successful classroom teaching and professional teacher conduct. It is not enough to be able to name the goal of the lesson and to know what the lesson plan says, because these goals are too abstract and too far removed from one's own classroom. Such goals tend to focus on the what, which is insufficient. To achieve this, it is recommended in *Visible Learning* that two goals be set for most lessons – one for the surface or content and the other for the deep level of relations desired between ideas. These types of understanding can be associated with the difficulty levels "Reproduction" and "Reorganization" on the one hand and "Transfer" and "Problem solving" on the other, as introduced by the German Council of Education (1970). Alternatively, the SOLO model ("Structure of observed learning outcomes") developed by John Biggs and Kevin Collis (1982) or the model "Depth of Knowledge" (DOK) by Norman L. Webb (1997) may be used (Table 10.1).

A closer look shows that the similarities between SOLO and the DOK level are greater than the differences. In particular, it becomes evident that these difficulty levels can be connected to "Piagetian programs" (d = 1.28) mentioned earlier. If a student has not yet developed a surface understanding (reproduction and reorganization) of the subject matter, attempting to complete tasks at the level of a deep understanding

TABLE 10.1

	GERMAN COUNCIL OF EDUCATION (1970)	SOLO (1982)	DOK (1997)
Surface level	Reproduction	Unistructural	Recall and reproduction
	Reorganization	Multistructural	Skills and concepts
Deep level	Transfer	Relational level	Strategic thinking and reasoning
	Problem solving	Extended abstract level	Extended thinking

(transfer and problem solving) may not make sense. Conversely, for a student who already has a deep understanding (transfer and problem solving), it is not sufficiently stimulating to deal with tasks at the level of surface understanding (reproduction and reorganization).

6. Mindframe: I offer and help students understand feedback and I interpret and act on feedback given to me

The question of effectiveness and subsequently the question of proving that effectiveness is a key point for Visible Learning and successful teaching. An essential factor in this is so-called "backward design" – literally moving backward. What this means is that an evaluation of classroom teaching must be thought out from the end: After the lesson is before the lesson. The goal to be achieved must be the starting point. We will use the example of the factor "Feedback" (d = 0.70) to demonstrate this method.

Successful feedback depends on clear goals and asks the questions "Where are you going?", "How are you getting there?", and "Where to next?" In this respect, successful feedback entails completion of the steps "Task", "Process", and "Self-regulation". Various studies have shown that this is a rare occurrence, and that focus on self-regulation hardly ever happens, even though it is the most important aspect of feedback for learners.

The following questions may help you reflect on your own feedback practices as a teacher and improve them.

Task

- Does the student's answer match the success criteria?
- Is the answer true or false?
- How can the answer be formulated in more detail?
- What part of the answer is true or false?
- What is missing that would make the answer comprehensive?

Process

- What strategies were used in the learning process?
- What worked well in the learning process and what could be improved?

- What are the strengths and weaknesses of the learning process?
- What further information is provided in completing the task with regard to the learning process?

Self-regulation

- What goals does the student consider he or she has achieved?
- What reasons does the student give for having solved a task correctly or incorrectly?
- How does the student explain his or her success?
- What are the next goals and tasks?
- How can the student self-direct and monitor the learning process?

Due to the dialogic structure of feedback it is worth mentioning that feedback from the students to the teacher is also important. Were they able to work with the methods? Were the media practicable and suitable? Was the organization helpful? And was the teacher's presentation clear and correct? A feedback target may be used to obtain this information (Figure 10.4). The closer the feedback is to the center, the better it is.

This procedure may be adapted where necessary. For instance, you can limit the assessment to only two dimensions (see Figure 10.5). This gives you a feedback system of coordinates where the assessment is better, the further it is to the outside.

It should not be forgotten that there are procedures using new media, such as computers, tablets, etc. When used correctly these devices can reveal findings that are difficult or impossible to make visible without them – further proof that new media are not a self-starter but need people to make an impact. Apart from possible costs, the advantage of new media in this context is that their use enables more complex feedback with less work. For example, it is quick and easy to offer learners a comprehensive questionnaire with the help of an app (e.g., www.feedbackschule.de) and to have it evaluated in seconds at the click of a mouse. This creates time and space for the decisive step of feedback: The conversation with learners.

Since we know that successful teachers are not lone warriors but work together with other teachers, we will now look at a third form of feedback: Feedback from teacher to teacher. Studies have determined that in the course of a week, teachers talk about everything other than their own teaching practices: About learners, about parents, about colleagues,

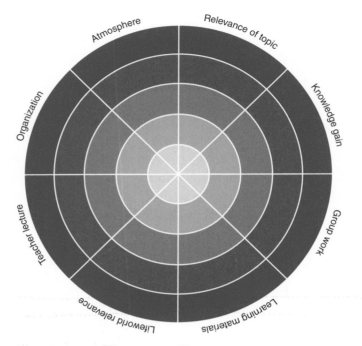

FIGURE 10.4 Feedback target

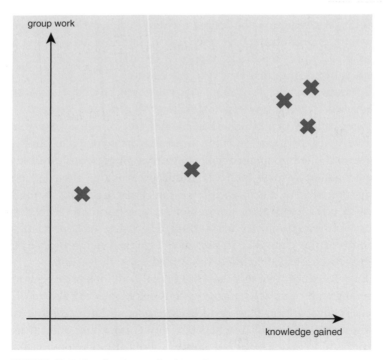

FIGURE 10.5 Feedback coordinate system

but hardly ever about their own teaching and even less about the impact of their teaching. This may be due in part to superficial relationships among teachers who are not yet ready for such in-depth exchanges about their own teaching and therefore their own personality. It certainly points to the importance of school leaders deciding on the appropriate narrative and building trust in the staffroom to enable powerful discussions among teachers about their impact. A certain measure of caution is therefore prudent when introducing feedback processes that presuppose a certain degree of feedback culture. If a school tries, for instance, to introduce team observations among colleagues, the teaching staff must already have developed a positive mindframe towards such measures to enable a climate of mutual trust. If this is not the case, important steps towards change can fail before they have even begun.

Subsequently, we will make a few practical recommendations. First, talking with one another precedes talking about one another. Second, approving feedback makes critical feedback easier. Third, feedback occurs at different levels (classroom, staff, administration, authority). The way from the inside (classroom) to the outside (authority) appears to be more effective with regard to developing a feedback culture. It is obvious that a feedback culture depends on a corresponding mindframe: Mistakes are not seen as deficits, but as opportunities. Teaching is understood to be a dialogue and not a monologue. The teacher–student relationship is based on mutual trust and confidence, and the development of a feedback culture – as with any other culture – takes time and cannot be introduced overnight.

7. Mindframe: I engage as much in dialogue as in monologue

According to current research, cooperative forms of learning ($d = 0.47$) have proven to be particularly effective – especially when they are used in combination with direct instruction ($d = 0.45$) and lead to clarity regarding goals, content, methods, and media on the part of learners and teachers. Cooperative learning is based on the three-step process "Think" – "Pair" – "Share" and can be illustrated using the example of a "Group puzzle" shown in Figure 10.6.

In this activity, the class is first divided into expert groups. Within these groups, everyone must work individually on part of the subject matter of the lesson (Think). After that, the expert groups share and discuss the results of the individual work (Pair). Finally, the class is brought back together and new groups are formed with one member

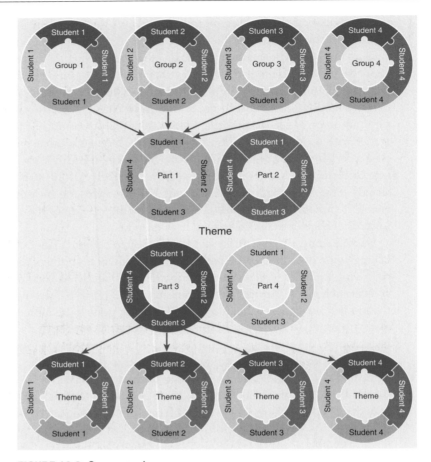

FIGURE 10.6 Group puzzle

from each expert group. The students report to one another on the results worked out in their expert groups (Share).

8. Mindframe: I explicitly inform students what successful impact looks like from the outset

For learners, it is doubtlessly helpful to know when they have reached the learning goal and the success criteria. Teaching in which the success criteria of learning are not touched upon is a lost opportunity. There are certainly several ways to reach the learning goal. However, the disclosure of the success criteria no later than when the goal is achieved is essential for successful and sustainable learning. But it depends on the teachers whether they wish to inform students what successful impact looks like from the outset.

Learning intentions and success criteria are two sides of the same coin and are mutually dependent on each other regarding their effect. The explication of the one criterion is, therefore, worthwhile especially when the other criterion is also made visible. The difference between the two is that, at the beginning of the learning process, learning objectives reveal what the goal of learning is and success criteria make visible when this learning goal is achieved.

Against this background, it is important not only for teachers to know what the goal of the lesson is and when it has been achieved but also to share this knowledge with the learner and to make it the explicit subject of the lesson.

Figure 10.7 tries to illustrate the interactions and the interrelations between learning intentions and success criteria. For this purpose, a teaching example is selected and worked through using the SOLO model, which has already been addressed.

9. Mindframe: I build relationships and trust so that learning can occur in a place where it is safe to make mistakes and learn from others

An open error culture as described above can only emerge based on intact "Teacher–student relationships" ($d = 0.63$). An atmosphere of trust and confidence, safety, care, and goodwill is essential for education in general and student achievement in particular. This requires

Unistructural/ multistructural	Recognize that light/sound are forms of energy and have properties	I can name one or more properties of light/sound	❑
Relational	Know that sound/light can be transformed into other forms of energy	I can explain how light/sound is transformed into other types of energy	❑
Extended abstract	Understand how light/sound allows us to communicate	I can discuss how light/sound enables us to communicate	❑

FIGURE 10.7 An example of learning intentions and success criteria categorized by the SOLO model

"student-centered" and "passionate" teachers who are primarily concerned with their students and not with their own knowledge and skills. The learners thus become the starting point of the teaching process. Their success becomes the teachers' success. The dominant mindframe is that teaching is something that is done together, and both sides need one another. Failure of the learning process is not ascribed (exclusively) to the learners but is seen as a joint failure that at the same time presents the necessity and opportunity to try and try again.

10. Mindframe: I focus on learning and the language of learning

One core message from *Visible Learning* is that considering prior knowledge and experience is important for successful classroom teaching. Think back to the factor "Piagetian programs" with an effect size of $d = 1.28$. This leads us to the task of examining the learning conditions and to decide:

■ What is the achievement level of the learners? Are they beginners, advanced, or experts?

■ What is the level of learners' conviction of their own effectiveness? Is it high so that difficult tasks are seen as a challenge? Or is it low so that difficult tasks are seen as a threat?

■ What is the level of motivation? Do learners self-motivate (intrinsic) or does motivation come from external factors (extrinsic)?

At this point we would like to express a cautionary note about widely used tests for determining learners' visual, acoustic, tactile, or other learning styles. *Visible Learning* shows that these styles often lack quality. They usually do not measure what they think they measure, so they provide unclear results that benefit the publisher more than the learner. The message is more about understanding the learning strategies students have, and not about classifying students into preferred styles of learning.

It would be a simplification to make teachers solely responsible for their students' learning success. The average effect sizes of the nine domains "Student", "Home", "School", "Classroom", "Teacher", "Curriculum", "Teaching strategies", "Learning strategies", and "Implementation methods" from *Visible Learning* demonstrate this fact, as does the major impact of "socioeconomic status" (d = 0.56) or "deep motivation and approach" (d = 0.71). Learning is not undertaken by individuals but requires close exchange between all parties involved in the process. Certainly, teachers as experts in education and classroom teaching play a key role, since it is their task to transfer the "language of the school" to the "language of parents" and to the "language of learners".

These considerations and processes can be important building blocks for working on your own mindframes. Another important step is self-reported grades – according to *Visible Learning*, this factor has one of the highest effect sizes: 1.22. Among the essential elements of teacher professionalism are to become aware of how one thinks about what one does, why one does what one does, and to reflect critically/constructively on one's actions. The factor "collective teacher efficacy" with the highest effect size of 1.57 indicates that these processes are more effective within a team than when each person goes through them on their own. As a result, it is worthwhile becoming aware of the prevailing attitudes in the college and to enter into an exchange. The questionnaire shown in Table 10.2 can be a first step.

TABLE 10.2

	STRONGLY AGREE	AGREE	DISAGREE	STRONGLY DISAGREE
I am an evaluator of my impact on student learning.	❏	❏	❏	❏
I see assessment as informing my impact and next steps.	❏	❏	❏	❏
I collaborate with my peers and my students about my concepts of progress and my impact.	❏	❏	❏	❏
I am a change agent and believe all students can improve.	❏	❏	❏	❏
I strive for challenge and not merely "doing one's best".	❏	❏	❏	❏

(Continued)

TABLE 10.2 (Continued)

	STRONGLY AGREE	AGREE	DISAGREE	STRONGLY DISAGREE
I offer and help students understand feedback, and I interpret and act on feedback given to me.	❏	❏	❏	❏
I engage as much in dialogue as in monologue.	❏	❏	❏	❏
I explicitly inform students what successful impact looks like from the outset.	❏	❏	❏	❏
I build relationships and trust so that learning can occur in a place where it is safe to make mistakes and to learn from others.	❏	❏	❏	❏
I focus on learning and the language of learning.	❏	❏	❏	❏

Starting with this list, you can query your own mindframes, make your own teaching practices visible, and develop them in conversations with your colleagues: "Know thy impact!"

References

Biggs, J., & Collis, K. (1982). *Evaluating the quality of learning: The SOLO taxonomy.* New York: Academic Press.

German Council of Education (Ed.) (1970). *Strukturplan für das Bildungswesen.* Stuttgart: Klett.

Hattie, J., & Zierer, K. (2018). *10 mindframes for Visible Learning. Teaching for success.* Abingdon, Oxon: Routledge.

Sinek, S. (2009). *Start with why: How great leaders inspire everyone to take action.* New York: Penguin.

Webb, N. (1997). *Research monograph number 6: Criteria for alignment of expectations and assessments on mathematics and science education.* Washington, DC: CCSSO.

FAQs

In the following, we have compiled a series of questions which we are asked again and again and which represent exemplary highlights and pitfalls in the discussion of "*Visible Learning*". We have tried to answer them as briefly and as concisely as possible. In this respect, no claim is made to completeness. Our goal is rather to aim for clarity and address common ambiguities. For this purpose, the questions are divided into "General", "Research basics", "Effect size", "Student achievement", "Meta-analysis", "Class size", "Homework", "Leadership", "Teacher", and "Student".

General

1. What is "*Visible Learning*"?

"*Visible Learning*" is a synthesis of meta-analyses and was first published in book form in 2008 after 15 years of work by John Hattie. This edition included approximately 800 meta-analyses, and has been claimed to contain the largest data set of empirical educational research ever evaluated. This work continues to this day, so that the current data set contains over 1,400 meta-analyses. The most important works in the context of "*Visible Learning*" are: *Visible Learning* (2008), *Visible Learning for Teachers* (2013), *Visible Learning and the Science of How We Learn* (2014), *Visible Learning into Action* (2015), and *10 Mindframes for Visible Learning* (2017). Two more recent books are *Developing Assessment-Capable Visible Learners* (2018) and *Visible Learning: Feedback* (2019).

There are also books which convert the ideas into practice: *Visible Learning in Literacy* (2016), *Visible Learning in Mathematics* (2017), *Visible Learning in Science* (2018), *Teaching Science in the Visible Learning*

Classroom (2018), *Visible Learning: Feedback* (2018), and *Visible Learning for English Language Learners* (2019). There are also associated work books, and companion books for elementary and high school in each subject.

2. How should I use *Visible Learning* as a teacher?

The book serves as a *basis for discussion* on using evidence to inform your school's practice. One example might be on how feedback can be modified within the classroom. This can assist teachers to optimize their feedback and heighten students' awareness of the benefits of effective feedback. It also creates awareness of *how* feedback might be getting through to students. In this way, the mindframes of learners and teachers are always taken into account.

3. What barriers are there to *Visible Learning*?

Visible Learning has been very well received by many teachers. Nevertheless, it cannot be denied that there have also been misunderstandings. These are often based on a superficial and abridged consideration of the results obtained. Openness to the *Visible Learning* approach is therefore essential if schools are to be able to change successfully. If this is the case, according to our experience, *Visible Learning* is convincing due to the clarity of positions and results.

Research basics

1. Why is the research focused on one dimension of schooling (i.e., student achievement)?

Visible Learning is based on quantitative empirical primary studies that typically target the performance area expected in school contexts: mathematical, scientific, and linguistic competencies that are measured by means of standardized tests or state performance comparisons. This emphasis is thus a mirror image of the emphasis on primary studies. Other target dimensions of school education, such as social behavior, moral judgment, or democracy education, are no less important, but are not at the heart of *Visible Learning*.

2. How do you allow for variability in design and quality for the studies gathered in the *Visible Learning* handbook? How can I be sure that the results are robust?

Other scientists have studied this question and found that the quality of meta-analyses is generally less important. It becomes more significant when the effect size is very small (<.10). This result is essentially confirmed in *Visible Learning*. Nevertheless, lower quality meta-analyses may and have been discarded.

3. Many of the main issues covered in the book – student feedback, linking prior and subsequent learning, going from known to unknown – are from the early 1970s. Am I running the risk of just repeating old ideas?

Empirical educational research is always a look into the past. The studies in *Visible Learning* are mainly from the 1990s to 2010s. *Visible Learning* is a literature review based on analyses of the past. It is also worth noting, however, that not all convincing and successful ideas from the 1970s are currently shared by all colleagues. There is no correlation between the size of the effect and publication year of the studies.

4. Most of the studies in the book were carried out in highly developed English-speaking countries. Is the research therefore applicable to non-English-speaking, non-Western countries?

Yes, it is indeed the case that many of the studies are from developed countries, and generalizing to other countries needs caution. Relative to high-income countries, academic achievement in low-income countries can be affected more by students' social status and variations at the school level, and less by teacher quality. It is for this reason that it is not recommended that this research is used in developing, non-Western countries. From our point of view, the dominance of English language is less important, since educational research today is international.

5. The table of "effect sizes" in the book clearly identifies the effects of one element and the effect size of another on student achievement, but what consideration is given

to the inter-correlation between those areas identified? As one example, teacher–student relationships has an effect size of d = 0.63, and reducing class size an effect size of only d = 0.14. However, what effect does reducing class size have on the ability of teachers to develop deeper relationships with their students?

We agree that the overlap between areas is critical. It is not as simple as combining the influences to get an increased effect. It is important to create a story about the underlying common parts such as success factors, student assessment capabilities, knowing thy impact, etc. This is why it took so long to write *Visible Learning* – it was understanding the story in the overlapping of so many influences.

Effect size

1. How is an effect size calculated?

Different methods are used to calculate an effect size. In *Visible Learning* Cohen's "d" is used (i.e., the mean difference of the measured values between a pre-test and a post-test or a intervention group compared to a control group, divided by the pooled standard deviation across both groups).

2. Why do you use an effect size of d = 0.40 as a cut-off point, basically ignoring effect sizes lower than d = 0.40?

Effect sizes below $d = 0.40$ are not ignored and it is also worth taking a closer look here. After all, understanding why a factor has low impact is often the prerequisite for increasing its effectiveness. However, a decision has been made to not look at what works ($0 < d < 0.40$) but what works best ($d > 0.40$). Ninety percent of all effect sizes in education are positive ($d > 0$) and this means that almost everything works. The effect size of $d = 0.4$ looks at the effects of innovations in achievement in such a way that we can notice real-world and more powerful differences. It is not a magical number but a guideline to initiate discussion about what we can aim for if we want to see change in students.

3. What is the preferred timescale over which an effect size can be calculated?

Work in schools and subsequent analyses indicate that a minimum of an 8- to 12-week period is needed to show whether effects, if any, are detected using effect sizes.

4. Is there a bias when using effect sizes in favor of lower achieving students?

There may be a bias when the design of the test creates a ceiling which does not allow high achievers to make any progress.

5. What precautions should I take when calculating an effect size?

Effect sizes are more accurate when calculated from a large sample. Thus caution should be exercised when interpreting effect sizes from small samples (< 30). One should also be extra cautious when the sample group includes outliers (i.e., students with exceptionally high or low scores). When calculating an effect size it is best to compare your results including and excluding outliers to see if it makes a difference. When comparing pre-test and post-test scores, it is more useful to ensure that all students are tested and that scores from the same group of students are compared. Finally, one should always look at the context when interpreting effect sizes.

Student achievement

1. What defines "achievement"? Is it student results in standardized testing or are there other measures?

Achievement relates to the subjects typically taught in schools, with a preponderance in mathematics and reading (followed by science and social studies), and fewer in the Arts. In terms of *Visible Learning* research, there is a good mix of standardized tests, state tests, and researcher and teacher constructed tests.

2. Is it realistic to expect that the bottom 50 percent of learners will improve?

Yes. Our expectation is that all students can and will improve and show progress over the course of a year. The key is the mindframe that we as teachers are change agents and that so many teachers are successful at pointing students in positive directions.

Meta-analysis

1. What is meta-analysis?

Meta-analysis is the use of statistical methods to combine results of primary studies. In this case "*Visible Learning*" is a synthesis of meta-analyses and is oriented to the corresponding standards, although new approaches in statistical procedures have to be taken.

2. What are some of the common problems with the use of meta-analysis?

In short, there are three main issues with meta-analysis. First, you are comparing disparate studies, so care is needed to consider possible moderators to any overall conclusion. Second, meta-analysis is focussed on seeking averages, and thus it is important to allow for the variance or spread of results. Third, studies only report past findings.

3. Why does "*Visible Learning*" focus on averages, thereby ignoring the complexity of the classroom and the wide variety of results?

Classrooms are highly complex places. Although there are common themes, averages cannot do justice to this. This is why a major feature of meta-analysis is to provide the opportunity to assess the effects of moderators and the many factors that can influence an average. Nevertheless, empirical studies show that generalizability of the overall effect is possible because there are far fewer moderators than is generally assumed.

Class size

1. What are your thoughts about research which suggests that class size does not matter?

This view is not shared. Research in recent years has shown that reducing class size increases student achievement, but the impact is small. Compared to other factors it is a minor but positive effect. The key question is: "Why is the effect of class size so small, especially given the many claims that have been made about it and many share that it should be much larger?" Reducing class size can do a lot, but it's not a sure thing. What are needed are teachers who are able to make good use of the changed initial conditions. Thus, understanding the impact of class size can be important before deciding to invest in this intervention.

Homework

1. How important is homework in the *Visible Learning* research and is there a difference between primary/elementary and secondary/high school?

Yes. There is a difference between homework in primary ($d = 0.15$) and secondary education ($d = 0.64$) where the effect size is a lot higher in secondary education. Again, understanding why there is this difference is important and explored in *Visible Learning* (for example, homework offers the opportunity to practice something that has already been taught and is more effective than expecting students to learn new things at home – such as tackling new projects. More high school homework is practice which is partly why the effect is higher).

2. Are you recommending that homework be abolished in elementary/primary schools?

No. Schools need to consider the type of homework they give. The evidence hints that homework needs to be learned on the one hand, and, on the other, that homework as we traditionally see it in primary schools may have a low impact, so it is worth checking. Homework needs to be: linked to the lesson; monitored by the teacher; short in duration; and not include new learning, as this disadvantages those who most need the guidance of a professional teacher.

Leadership

1. What is the difference between transformational and instructional leaders?

Instructional leadership (d = 0.42) refers to those school leaders who focus on teaching and have high expectations of both teachers and learners. Transformational leadership (d = 0.12) refers to those school leaders who focus on an appreciative togetherness and a climate of well-being. If school leaders succeed in bringing both perspectives together to become a "collaborative leadership", they can achieve the greatest influence.

2. What can school leaders do to shift the mindframes of teachers and make a difference?

Lots, but let's concentrate on one. The evidence shows that if school leaders see themselves as "evaluators" then they are likely to have the highest chance of shifting the mindframes of teachers towards the greatest impact on student learning. These school leaders need to be clear about what it is that they want from their students and to be able to recognize the success indicators. Ask: How do I know this is working? How can I compare "this" with "that"? What is the merit and worth of this influence on learning? What is the magnitude of the effect? What evidence will convince you that you are wrong? Where is the evidence which shows that this is superior to other programs? Where have you seen this in practice so that it produces effective results? Do I share a common concept of progress? By developing evaluation plans about the impact of teaching and learning, your own effects can lead to others seeing the value of these questions, providing evidence about the impact on student learning and teachers' teaching, and creating a healthy respect for ensuring that it all makes a difference.

Teacher

1. What should I as an educator focus on?

The major theme of *Visible Learning* is: Know thy impact! This is what we would like educators to focus on. In a nutshell: Everything works. So asking whether X improves achievement is a trivial claim. We need to aim for a larger magnitude of change than just "any change" and we know what is average (d = <0.40), so this is the minimal target. The key is for school leaders, systems, and teachers to understand the impact they are making and to work from this. If it is less than d = 0.40 you have to ask yourself: Is it worthwhile carrying on? If it is more than d = 0.40 then carry on with what you are doing. "Know thy impact!" forces the moral question: Impact on what? This is more than achievement. This extends to making schools inviting places to learn, retention through to the final year of school, moving from surface only to include deep processing, enjoyment, passion, etc.

2. How can we change teachers' thinking about what effects are most significant in a child's learning? How can we change the mindframes of teachers?

This is indeed not an easy task – but should we shy away from it, especially since we know how influential attitudes are? In numerous projects we have come to the conclusion that it is possible to change attitudes, even if it is not easy. This requires, first, raising awareness of attitudes, and, second, making them visible. Third, empirical evidence can then be cited, which may lead to confirmation or irritation – both lead in turn to profound professionalization processes, which can finally be made conscious and visible again.

3. How does the teacher's preparation (i.e. planning and preparing lessons) affect the students' learning progress?

The likelihood of learning progress increases with sound and well-considered lesson planning. The main aim is for teachers to plan their teaching cooperatively and with particular emphasis on sharing the criteria of success with the students. So we don't just suggest more time for planning, especially when this happens in isolation (or, worse, when you sit with other teachers in the staffroom and still work alone). We are committed to focussed collective lesson planning in light of the past and expected impact on the students as a result of that planning. We know this is not easy, but it is a key element of successful schools.

Student

1. If students are all achieving different targets, what sorts of learning intentions do we need to set?

The effects are stronger at the individual level, but the ways of setting and monitoring targets can be taught as a class unit. To manage this effectively, students who have common targets can be taught as a small group. Targets are often set around a common need which allows the teacher to set a more global learning intention and differentiate through the success criteria. For example, the whole class may need to focus on punctuation, with one group of students learning to use capital letters and full stops correctly and another group learning to use semicolons and commas for phrasing.

2. What effect does digital media have on students' learning?

The potential of digital media is currently being discussed in many places and in many layers. Some voices even speak of a "digital revolution" in education. The claim that digital media are attractive to both teachers and learners and command much more attention than other resources in the classroom may be true at first glance. At second glance, however, it becomes apparent that these effects recede after a certain period of time. This proves that digital media cannot be taken for granted. Against this background, it is not surprising that many primary studies come to the conclusion that digital media rarely have a resounding effect on student achievement. The reasons are manifold. Our view is that they are often only used as a substitute for traditional media and that their intrinsic potential can rarely be expressed. Only if teachers change their teaching to optimize the performance of digital media will there be an increased effect: Pedagogy before technology.

B

250-plus factors (May 2018)

In order to gain an overview of all domains and factors that have been compiled and evaluated in *Visible Learning* up to May 2018, a corresponding overview is given below. It is based on over 1,400 meta-analyses and comprises a total of 255 factors. These are assigned to the domains "Student", "Home", "School", "Classroom", "Curricula", "Teacher", "Teaching strategies", "Implementation methods", and "Learning strategies", and are arranged in alphabetical order. In view of the risk of an abbreviated interpretation, it should be noted that factors cannot be seen independently of one another, but are interdependent and may have a far-reaching cost–benefit ratio. All this must be taken into account when looking at the overview. In this sense, it serves primarily for orientation.

Student

FACTOR	d	N-METAS	N-STUDIES	AGE-MIN	AGE-MAX	SE-METAS	d (WEIGHTED)
Achieving motivation and approach	0.44	2	113	1999	1999	0.22	0.62
ADHD	-0.90	1	31	2015	2015	0.00	-0.90
Anxiety	0.42	8	254	1987	2015	0.07	-0.37
Attitude to content domains	0.35	4	320	1983	2010	0.04	0.38
Boredom	-0.49	1	29	2015	2015	0.00	-0.49
Breastfeeding	0.04	1	12	2006	2006	0.00	0.04
Concentration/persistence/engagement	0.56	2	44	1991	2004	0.39	0.42
Creativity and achievement	0.40	2	141	2005	2016	0.04	0.44
Deafness	-0.61	1	12	2016	2016	0.00	-0.61
Deep motivation and approach	0.69	2	110	1999	1999	0.04	0.71
Depression	-0.36	2	70	2013	2013	0.04	-0.35
Drugs (ADHD)	0.32	8	411	1975	2008	0.05	0.41
Exercise/relaxation	0.26	8	397	1985	2014	0.05	0.25
Field independence	0.68	2	46	2005	2009	0.20	0.55
Gender	0.08	30	2441	1980	2015	0.05	0.02
Grit/incremental vs. entity thinking	0.25	2	173	2013	2016	0.04	0.25
Lack of illness	0.26	7	121	1983	2013	0.05	0.27
Lack of sleep	-0.05	3	96	2010	2015	0.11	0.01

Lack of stress	0.17	1	26	2016	2016	0.00	0.17
Mastery goals	0.06	6	379	2007	2014	0.07	0.10
Mindfulness	0.29	3	66	2012	2014	0.05	0.30
Morning vs. eveningness	0.12	3	267	2011	2015	0.13	0.08
Non-standard dialect use	-0.29	1	19	2015	2015	0.00	-0.29
Performance goals	-0.01	6	360	2007	2014	0.06	0.06
Personality	0.26	19	1004	1983	2016	0.05	0.21
Piagetian programs	1.28	1	51	1981	1981	0.00	1.28
Positive ethnic self-identity	0.12	4	111	1999	2016	0.19	0.16
Pre-term birth weight	-0.57	7	148	2002	2014	0.05	-0.58
Prior ability	0.94	7	1540	1981	2015	0.12	0.82
Prior achievement	0.55	5	206	1988	2007	0.07	0.54
Relationship of high school achievement to adult performance	0.38	2	147	1985	1989	0.01	0.37
Relationship of high school to university achievement	0.60	5	2061	1990	2012	0.14	0.53
Relative age within a class	0.45	1	8	2013	2013	0.00	0.45
Self-concept	0.41	7	467	1980	2015	0.03	0.43
Self-efficacy	0.92	4	122	1990	2007	0.29	0.77
Self-reported grades	1.33	7	250	1982	2011	0.33	1.22
Stereotype threat	0.33	2	95	2014	2016	0.30	0.08
Surface motivation and approach	-0.11	3	392	1999	2010	0.19	0.03
Working memory	0.64	9	503	1987	2016	0.07	0.67

Home

FACTOR	d	N-METAS	N-STUDIES	AGE-MIN	AGE-MAX	SE-METAS	d (WEIGHTED)
Adopted children	0.25	3	150	1993	2011	0.08	0.21
Corporal punishment in the home	-0.33	1	16	2004	2004	0.00	-0.33
Divorced or remarried	0.23	8	395	1984	2007	0.05	0.28
Fathers	0.20	6	324	1987	2014	0.05	0.22
Home environment	0.52	3	48	1982	2007	0.11	0.53
Home visiting	0.29	2	71	1996	2004	0.09	0.22
Immigrant status	0.01	1	53	2016	2016	0.00	0.01
Military deployment	-0.16	1	5	2011	2011	0.00	-0.16
Mobility	-0.34	3	181	1989	1997	0.07	-0.39
Other family structure	0.16	4	231	1986	2013	0.04	0.18
Parental autonomy support	0.15	3	258	2008	2015	0.03	0.14
Parental employment	0.03	2	88	2007	2010	0.03	0.05
Parental involvement	0.50	15	883	1983	2015	0.07	0.42
Socioeconomic status	0.52	7	622	1982	2011	0.05	0.56
Television	-0.18	3	37	1982	2001	0.04	-0.15
Welfare policies	-0.12	1	8	2004	2004	0.00	-0.12

School

FACTOR	d	N-METAS	N-STUDIES	AGE-MIN	AGE-MAX	SE-METAS	d (WEIGHTED)
Charter schools	0.09	4	263	2001	2015	0.05	0.03
Collective teacher efficacy	1.57	1	26	2011	2011	0.00	1.57
College halls of residence	0.05	1	10	1999	1999	0.00	0.05
Desegregation	0.28	10	335	1980	1989	0.08	0.23
Different types of early intervention	0.29	8	331	1986	2010	0.05	0.27
Diversity of students	0.10	3	55	2010	2013	0.03	0.09
Early intervention	0.44	3	312	1993	1999	0.09	0.48
Early intervention in the home	0.27	4	123	1994	2010	0.06	0.23
External accountability systems	0.31	1	14	2008	2008	0.00	0.31
Finances	0.21	6	228	1986	2016	0.09	0.19
Head start programs	0.33	6	412	1983	2013	0.04	0.37
Middle school interventions	0.08	1	38	2011	2011	0.00	0.08
Out-of-school curricula experiences	0.12	4	100	2003	2014	0.05	0.11
Pre-school programs	0.26	12	648	1983	2016	0.07	0.30

(Continued)

School (Continued)

FACTOR	d	N-METAS	N-STUDIES	AGE-MIN	AGE-MAX	SE-METAS	d (WEIGHTED)
Pre-school with at-risk students	0.56	9	1018	1983	2004	0.08	0.52
Principals/school leaders	0.32	16	555	1991	2015	0.09	0.28
Religious schools	0.24	3	127	2002	2012	0.02	0.23
School choice	0.12	1	22	2017	2017	0.00	0.12
School climate	0.32	9	427	2009	2016	0.06	0.31
School effects	0.48	1	168	1997	1997	0.00	0.48
School size	0.43	1	21	1991	1991	0.00	0.43
Single-sex schools	0.08	1	184	2014	2014	0.00	0.08
Summer school	0.23	3	105	2000	2002	0.03	0.22
Summer vacation	−0.02	2	78	1996	2003	0.05	−0.02
Suspension/expelling students	−0.20	1	24	2015	2015	0.00	−0.20

Classroom

FACTOR	d	N-METAS	N-STUDIES	AGE-MIN	AGE-MAX	SE-METAS	d (WEIGHTED)
Ability grouping	0.12	14	500	1982	2001	0.03	0.11
Ability grouping for gifted students	0.30	5	125	1985	1992	0.09	0.20
Acceleration	0.68	3	75	1984	2011	0.17	0.58
Background music	0.10	2	79	2010	2010	0.10	0.08
Class size	0.21	4	113	1997	2009	0.06	0.14
Classroom behavior	0.62	5	252	1990	2014	0.13	0.60
Classroom cohesion	0.44	4	104	1980	2007	0.16	0.53
Classroom management	0.35	2	154	2003	2016	0.13	0.40
Cognitive behavioral programs	0.29	1	5	2013	2013	0.00	0.29
Counseling effects	0.35	7	367	1998	2012	0.13	0.29
Decreasing disruptive behavior	0.34	3	165	1985	2004	0.45	0.59
Detracking	0.09	1	15	2010	2010	0.00	0.09
Enrichment	0.53	4	240	1989	2016	0.14	0.53
Mainstreaming/inclusion	0.27	8	197	1980	2016	0.07	0.36
Mentoring	0.12	4	152	2007	2012	0.05	0.17
Multi-grade/multi-age classes	0.04	3	94	1995	1998	0.05	0.04
Not being liked in class	−0.19	2	38	2009	2010	0.05	−0.23
Open vs. traditional	0.01	4	315	1980	1982	0.05	0.02

(Continued)

Classroom (Continued)

FACTOR	d	N-METAS	N-STUDIES	AGE-MIN	AGE-MAX	SE-METAS	d (WEIGHTED)
Peer influences	0.53	1	12	1980	1980	0.00	0.53
Retention	-0.32	9	255	1983	2011	0.07	-0.30
School calendars/timetables	0.09	1	47	2003	2003	0.00	0.09
Small group learning	0.47	7	209	1997	2017	0.03	0.45
Within class grouping	0.18	3	144	1985	2010	0.02	0.16

Curricula

FACTOR	d	N-METAS	N-STUDIES	AGE-MIN	AGE-MAX	SE-METAS	d (WEIGHTED)
Bilingual programs	0.36	12	371	1984	2016	0.10	0.53
Career interventions	0.38	3	143	1983	1992	0.09	0.34
Chess	0.34	1	24	2016	2016	0.00	0.34
Comprehension programs	0.47	20	878	1985	2016	0.06	0.48
Comprehensive instruction	0.72	14	495	1980	2014	0.17	0.93
Conceptual change programs	0.99	2	112	1993	2010	0.13	0.94
Creativity programs	0.62	14	817	1984	2016	0.06	0.65
Diversity courses	0.09	1	307	2017	2017	0.00	0.09
Drama/Arts programs	0.38	12	756	1987	2016	0.06	0.41
Exposure to reading	0.43	13	466	1995	2013	0.06	0.48

Extra-curricular programs	0.20	12	293	1997	2014	0.05	0.22
Integrated/curricular programs	0.47	3	89	2000	2011	0.07	0.46
Juvenile delinquent programs	0.12	1	15	2012	2012	0.00	0.12
Manipulative materials on mathematics	0.30	6	274	1983	2013	0.08	0.33
Mathematics programs	0.59	26	1112	1978	2017	0.08	0.53
Motivation programs	0.34	4	175	1985	2016	0.06	0.36
Music-based reading programs	0.37	2	50	2008	2013	0.04	0.36
Outdoor/adventure programs	0.43	4	194	1994	2008	0.09	0.49
Perceptual-motor programs	0.08	1	180	1983	1983	0.00	0.08
Phonics instruction	0.70	25	931	1988	2015	0.13	0.86
Repeated reading programs	0.75	4	106	2002	2015	0.14	0.9
Science	0.48	19	1193	1979	2015	0.05	0.44
Second-/third-chance programs	0.53	3	68	2000	2016	0.09	0.47
Sentence-combining programs	0.15	2	35	1991	1993	0.04	0.13
Social skills programs	0.39	11	602	1987	2014	0.07	0.44
Spelling programs	0.58	1	91	2013	2013	0.00	0.58
Tactile stimulation programs	0.58	1	19	1987	1987	0.00	0.58
Use of calculators	0.27	5	222	1986	2006	0.06	0.23
Visual perception programs	0.55	6	683	1980	2000	0.13	0.66
Vocabulary programs	0.62	12	487	1982	2013	0.07	0.66
Whole language	0.06	4	64	1989	2000	0.23	0.13
Writing programs	0.45	11	538	1984	2016	0.06	0.45

Teacher

FACTOR	d	N-METAS	N-STUDIES	AGE-MIN	AGE-MAX	SE-METAS	d (WEIGHTED)
Microteaching	0.88	4	402	1981	1993	0.15	1.01
Professional development	0.41	18	1125	1980	2016	0.05	0.49
Student rating of quality of teaching	0.50	6	152	1980	2008	0.05	0.49
Teacher clarity	0.75	3	195	1991	2015	0.09	0.75
Teacher credibility	0.90	1	51	2009	2009	0.00	0.90
Teacher education	0.12	5	106	2004	2010	0.01	0.12
Teacher effects	0.32	1	18	2004	2004	0.00	0.32
Teacher estimates of achievement	1.29	2	108	2012	2016	0.25	1.42
Teacher expectations	0.43	8	674	1978	2007	0.09	0.57
Teacher performance pay	0.05	1	40	2017	2017	0.00	0.05
Teacher personality	0.25	4	56	1982	2017	0.03	0.26
Teacher subject matter knowledge	0.11	3	124	1983	2007	0.03	0.10
Teacher verbal ability	0.22	1	21	2009	2009	0.00	0.22
Teacher–student relationships	0.52	5	388	1984	2013	0.10	0.63
Teachers not labeling students	0.61	1	79	1985	1985	0.00	0.61
Teaching communication skills and strategies	0.43	1	23	2011	2011	0.00	0.43

Teaching strategies

FACTOR	d	N-METAS	N-STUDIES	AGE-MIN	AGE-MAX	SE-METAS	d (WEIGHTED)
Behavioral objectives/advance organizers	0.42	12	935	1978	2006	0.07	0.41
Classroom discussion	0.82	1	42	2011	2011	0.00	0.82
Cognitive task analysis	1.29	2	27	2004	2013	0.33	1.09
Concept mapping	0.64	9	1049	1984	2011	0.07	0.61
Feedback	0.70	31	1463	1980	2015	0.30	0.70
Goal commitment	0.40	3	103	1998	2011	0.04	0.44
Goal difficulty	0.59	6	375	1984	2004	0.05	0.60
Goal intentions	0.48	2	179	2007	2015	0.18	0.41
Goals	0.68	5	178	1986	2007	0.33	0.59
Learning hierarchies	0.19	1	24	1980	1980	0.00	0.19
Mastery learning	0.57	13	683	1976	1990	0.05	0.60
Peer tutoring	0.53	17	903	1977	2016	0.06	0.66
Planning and prediction	0.63	8	494	1987	2016	0.08	0.56
Providing formative evaluation	0.48	2	34	1986	2011	0.16	0.53
Questioning	0.48	8	241	1981	2009	0.08	0.46
Response to intervention	1.29	3	58	2005	2016	0.10	1.34
Setting standards for self-judgment	0.62	2	156	2008	2008	0.00	0.62
Types of testing	0.12	2	26	2000	2015	0.04	0.11
Volunteer tutors	0.26	1	21	2009	2009	0.00	0.26
Worked examples	0.37	2	83	2006	2010	0.16	0.47

Implementation methods

FACTOR	d	N-METAS	N-STUDIES	AGE-MIN	AGE-MAX	SE-METAS	d (WEIGHTED)
Adjunct aids	0.32	8	197	1981	2016	0.06	0.31
After-school programs	0.40	1	23	2011	2011	0.00	0.40
Clickers	0.22	2	81	2014	2016	0.13	0.17
Co-/team teaching	0.19	2	136	1983	2001	0.12	0.07
Collaborative learning	0.34	2	153	2009	2014	0.04	0.37
Competitive vs. individualistic learning	0.24	4	831	1981	2000	0.09	0.27
Comprehensive teaching reforms	0.28	4	88	1996	2013	0.09	0.25
Computer-assisted instruction	0.47	40	2474	1977	2016	0.04	0.41
Cooperative learning	0.40	19	579	1981	2015	0.04	0.47
Cooperative vs. competitive learning	0.53	8	1031	1981	2013	0.05	0.58
Cooperative vs. individualistic learning	0.55	5	959	1987	2013	0.11	0.62
Direct instruction	0.60	5	324	1988	2010	0.10	0.45
Discovery-based teaching	0.21	2	193	1987	2011	0.08	0.27
Distance education	0.13	15	901	1987	2011	0.04	0.11
Gaming/simulation	0.35	18	797	1981	2016	0.04	0.32
Home-school programs	0.16	1	14	2002	2002	0.00	0.16
Homework	0.28	7	206	1984	2017	0.05	0.32
Humor	0.04	1	20	2006	2006	0.00	0.04
Inductive teaching	0.44	3	206	1983	2013	0.18	0.58

Inquiry-based teaching	0.40	6	314	1983	2016	0.06	0.41
Intelligent tutoring systems	0.48	3	231	2013	2016	0.08	0.45
Interactive video methods	0.54	6	372	1980	2013	0.04	0.52
Interventions for students with learning needs	0.77	3	343	1996	1999	0.09	0.71
Jigsaw method	1.20	1	37	2014	2014	0.00	1.20
Mobile phones	0.35	4	254	2005	2017	0.05	0.39
One-on-one laptops	0.16	1	10	2016	2016	0.00	0.16
Online, digital tools	0.29	7	288	2008	2013	0.05	0.23
Philosophy in schools	0.43	1	10	2007	2007	0.00	0.43
Problem-based learning	0.26	15	585	1993	2016	0.09	0.33
Problem-solving teaching	0.68	11	683	1980	2011	0.07	0.59
Programmed instruction	0.23	8	493	1977	2000	0.04	0.24
Reciprocal teaching	0.74	2	38	1994	2003	0.00	0.74
Scaffolding	0.82	2	26	2012	2015	0.23	0.96
Service learning	0.58	3	39	2001	2012	0.13	0.55
Special college programs	0.21	5	429	1983	2014	0.07	0.26
Teaching creative thinking	0.34	2	458	2008	2015	0.01	0.33
Teaching strategies	0.57	16	5784	1983	2011	0.07	0.63
Technology in distance education	0.01	2	28	2003	2007	0.01	0.02
Technology in mathematics	0.33	18	865	1981	2014	0.04	0.31
Technology in other subjects	0.55	3	96	1992	2003	0.14	0.58
Technology in reading/literacy	0.29	15	652	2000	2015	0.04	0.25

(Continued)

Implementation methods (Continued)

FACTOR	d	N-METAS	N-STUDIES	AGE-MIN	AGE-MAX	SE-METAS	d (WEIGHTED)
Technology in science	0.23	6	391	1980	2007	0.04	0.18
Technology in small groups	0.21	3	193	2001	2004	0.05	0.17
Technology in writing	0.42	3	70	1991	2003	0.04	0.43
Technology with college students	0.42	11	2471	1980	2014	0.06	0.33
Technology with elementary students	0.44	6	264	1984	1993	0.04	0.44
Technology with high school students	0.30	9	681	1983	2009	0.01	0.30
Technology with learning needs students	0.57	4	114	1986	2003	0.09	0.62
Use of PowerPoint	0.26	1	12	2006	2006	0.00	0.26
Visual/audio-visual methods	0.22	6	359	1979	2000	0.10	0.10
Web-based learning	0.18	3	136	2002	2007	0.03	0.16

Learning strategies

FACTOR	d	N-METAS	N-STUDIES	AGE-MIN	AGE-MAX	SE-METAS	d (WEIGHTED)
Aptitude/treatment interactions	0.19	2	61	1987	1989	0.06	0.22
Deliberate practice	0.79	3	161	1983	2014	0.35	0.49
Effort management	0.77	1	15	2014	2014	0.00	0.77
Elaboration and organization	0.75	1	50	2014	2014	0.00	0.75
Elaborative interrogation	0.42	51	24	2013	2013	0.00	0.42
Evaluation and reflection	0.75	1	54	2014	2014	0.00	0.75
Help seeking	0.72	2	83	2008	2008	0.09	0.66
Imagery	0.45	1	12	2008	2008	0.00	0.45
Individualized instruction	0.23	12	670	1977	2010	0.04	0.23
Interleaved practice	0.21	1	12	2013	2013	0.00	0.21
Matching style of learning	0.31	13	685	1985	2016	0.08	0.31
Meta-cognitive strategies	0.58	7	450	1988	2015	0.05	0.52
Mnemonics	0.76	4	80	1987	2013	0.25	0.78
Note taking	0.50	7	160	1985	2016	0.09	0.41
Outlining and transforming	0.66	4	193	1999	2014	0.13	0.75
Practice testing	0.54	13	875	1984	2014	0.11	0.51
Record keeping	0.52	3	185	2008	2013	0.03	0.51
Rehearsal and memorization	0.73	3	132	1999	2014	0.30	0.57
Self-regulation strategies	0.52	7	701	2005	2013	0.06	0.45
Self-verbalization/self-questioning	0.55	9	463	1985	2013	0.06	0.62

(Continued)

Learning strategies (Continued)

FACTOR	d	N-METAS	N-STUDIES	AGE-MIN	AGE-MAX	SE-METAS	d (WEIGHTED)
Spaced vs. mass practice	0.42	1	24	2013	2013	0.00	0.42
Strategy monitoring	0.58	2	235	2008	2014	0.10	0.54
Strategy to integrate with prior knowledge	0.93	1	10	2008	2008	0.00	0.93
Student-centered teaching	0.36	3	349	2007	2014	0.09	0.35
Student control over learning	0.02	54	164	1992	2014	0.02	0.02
Study skills	0.46	11	659	1979	2013	0.08	0.46
Summarization	0.79	3	170	1985	2013	0.13	0.90
Task value	0.46	1	6	2010	2010	0.00	0.46
Teaching test taking and coaching	0.30	12	286	1981	2015	0.06	0.26
Time on task	0.44	11	326	1976	2014	0.11	0.50
Transfer strategies	0.86	5	211	2000	2013	0.16	0.75
Underlining and highlighting	0.50	1	16	2013	2013	0.00	0.50

Index

Page numbers in **bold** denote tables, those in *italics* denote figures.